THE
COMPLETE IDIOT'S GUIDE® TO

Finishing Your Basement

Illustrated

by Dan Ramsey

ALPHA

A member of Penguin Group (USA) Inc.

For Jude, my dedication.

Publisher: *Marie Butler-Knight*
Product Manager: *Phil Kitchel*
Senior Managing Editor: *Jennifer Chisholm*
Senior Acquisitions Editor: *Mike Sanders*
Development Editor: *Lynn Northrup*
Senior Production Editor: *Katherin Bidwell*
Copy Editor: *Susan Aufheimer*
Illustrator: *Chris Eliopoulos*
Cover/Book Designer: *Trina Wurst*
Indexer: *Julie Bess*
Layout/Proofreading: *Angela Calvert, Megan Douglass, Trina Wurst*

Contents at a Glance

Contents

Foreword

The best thing about finishing your basement is the freedom the space allows you. No where else in your home can you have so much creative license. I should know. I've finished 150 basements as a licensed contractor. Basements are the only projects I work on here in the Midwest. Most recently, my organization has been spotlighted by the local news for their feature on "Beautifying Your Basement." We've supplied content for magazine and newspaper articles as well. Over the years, you learn basements inside out and become an authority.

Dan Ramsey found me through my website as he was looking for photo help in the creation of this book. After reviewing the manuscript, I thought it interesting just how different basements are throughout the country. This was something I hadn't thought about before. Where I live, basements are typically sunk completely into the ground. Being dug by a backhoe, they're really just extensions of the foundation. It's not until after the homeowners have settled in that the reality enters in that here is a potential living space. Many times as contractors we have to contend with poorly placed mechanicals—furnaces, water heaters, and the like. It can be quite a challenge to accommodate them all. With some basements you really push the creative envelope.

In Dan's part of the country, along the West Coast, many basements are much different. Now this doesn't immediately mean the creative process is easier—it's just different. There, a "walkout" basement, as I would call it—a "daylight" basement to a West Coaster—is a common occurrence. We do have them here in the Midwest, but not very often. It's quite a treat for us when we do get to finish a walkout basement. Running materials in and out is less of a chore. In the Midwest, almost all of our supplies, tools, and trash go through the windows. Sheets of drywall and the doors are about the only things actually going up and down the stairs besides us.

After mentally viewing "the lay of the land," quite literally—I realize that walkouts are very common in other parts of the country, too. One such place is the Atlanta, Georgia, area. This is where my folks are. In fact, my parents' basement is a walkout. Many basements in newer homes in that region have the basement walls already studded. I noticed that as a result of this many of the homes don't require structural steel. What you're familiar with isn't always the way it is.

What it boils down to is that if I can learn something as a seasoned basement remodeler, you can, too. In *The Complete Idiot's Guide to Finishing Your Basement Illustrated*, Dan has captured the essence of the creative process and brought forth many other valuable points. Basement design is only one part of the basement equation. Don't simply limit yourself to walls and a ceiling. Figure out your needs and wants. Take the necessary time. Use this book! Then apply what you learn to your project. Follow Dan's guidance and create! You'll be glad you did.

Here's to a great basement!

—Dave Schrock
Owner, Dave's Dwellings, Inc.
www.basementideas.com

Introduction

Millions of homes across the United States and Canada have unfinished basements sitting underneath them. That's where the furnace system is. Or the home was sold with a "bonus area" to be finished later. Then life comes along with additional children, elderly parents who need care, teens who want their own space, an expanding home business, or need for additional income from a rental apartment. Where to turn? The unfinished basement, of course!

However, many folks feel that remodeling a basement is too big a job for them. They're intimidated by the task of turning an unfinished basement into useable living space. So the job gets put off. Where to start? Do I need a building permit? What about moisture? What about costs?

As a contractor and author, I've heard these questions many times. What are the answers? I'll tell you in this book. In fact, I'll *show* you. You'll see through the lens of my camera, and that of professional basement remodelers, what's needed and how to get it done.

The success of my previous book, *The Complete Idiot's Guide to Building Your Own Home* (Alpha Books, 2002), has proven that there is a real need for clear, step-by-step instructions on residential construction. The book you're holding, *The Complete Idiot's Guide to Finishing Your Basement Illustrated*, is aimed at doing the same for remodeling—with one very important addition: You'll find *lots* of photos and drawings. There are more than 300 of them in this book. Some are instructional and some are idea starters. All show you how to finish your own basement.

How to Use This Book

This book is presented in a very logical structure to make it easy to find things when you need them. Let's take a closer look at each part.

Part 1, "Planning Your Basement," helps you do just that. You'll get to see what's inside numerous finished basements without having to ring a doorbell. Your creative mind with be fed dozens of ideas, suggestions, tips, and caveats. Then you'll check out your own unfinished or partially finished basement and start making your own plans. Then back up to the kitchen where you'll sit down and figure out what it will all cost. Then you'll find out about building permits and stuff.

Part 2, "Remodeling Your Basement," puts a hammer in your hand. It shows you (with more than 190 photos and drawings) how to build and finish walls, install plumbing and fixtures, finish ceilings, install doors and windows, install flooring, and much more. It focuses on the special challenges that basements offer. Best of all, it's presented in terms that novice remodelers can apply.

Part 3, "Decorating Your Basement," puts the final touches on your new finished basement. It shows you how to add trim, paint and wallpaper, select and move in furniture, install security and other systems, and even how to furnish your new home office and other rooms.

In addition, you'll find an illustrated glossary at the back of the book that defines more than 200 terms, and a resources section that lists recommended books, websites, and more.

Extras

Along the way, practical sidebars will show you the safe and smart way to do things, define words and terms you may not be familiar with, point out any dangers or pitfalls, and give you other bits of helpful information. *The Complete Idiot's Guide to Finishing Your Basement Illustrated* makes the job easier— and maybe even fun!

On the Level

Three top-notch remodeling contractors share their tips and suggestions in these boxes, gleaned from many years of finishing basements.

Deeper Meaning

What does *that* mean? Here you'll find a concise definition of important basement remodeling terms in context. Also check the glossary in the back of this book for more definitions and even some photos to make things more clear.

Construction Zone

Don't get hurt! And don't let your wallet get hurt! Make sure you follow the cautions included in these boxes.

Things You Should Know

Here you'll find some other bits of valuable information that can help you finish your basement for less time and money.

Acknowledgments

Where to start?! Many qualified remodeling contractors, suppliers, and other experts have helped me develop—and illustrate—this book for you. They include:

Dave Schrock of Dave's Dwellings, Inc. of Aurora, Illinois, (www.basementideas.com) who supplied numerous photographs and extensive tips on finishing basements.

Brian Ellis of ECI Builders of Farmington Hills, Michigan, (www.ecibuilders.com) who provided valuable basement remodeling tips and many photos of finished jobs.

Greg Dunbar of Greg Dunbar Construction who guided the development of this book. Thanks again, Greg!

Bill Farmer of Mendo Mill, Willits, California, and Bob Doty of Mendo Mill, Ukiah, California, who shared tips as well as let me wander through their stores with my camera.

Robert Tyrrell, Heath Dowdy, Bob Wilson, and Jerry Goodrick of Hertz Big 4 Rents, Ukiah, California, for good advice and photo ops.

Richard Willey and Susan Philpot of Carpet One, Ukiah, California, for sharing product information and buying tips.

Frank Gunnink of Santa Rosa Tile Supply, Inc., Ukiah, California, for tips and pix.

Scott Harris of ART, Inc., developers of Chief Architect, for lending me their professional design software. It's a great tool!

Once again, a special thanks to Mike Sanders whose vision initiated this new visual step-by-step approach to practical how-to books. Last, but never least, a special thank-you to Lynn Northrup, Susan Aufheimer, and Kathy Bidwell, who make me a better writer than I really am.

Trademarks

All terms mentioned in this book that are known to be or are suspected of being trademarks or service marks have been appropriately capitalized. Alpha Books and Penguin Group (USA) Inc. cannot attest to the accuracy of this information. Use of a term in this book should not be regarded as affecting the validity of any trademark or service mark.

In This Part

Part 1

Planning Your Basement

It's a fact: Every minute spent planning saves many minutes of work. Because I'm basically lazy, I've applied this fact on a wide variety of remodeling projects and proven it to be true. I'd much rather spend time doodling, er, planning than actually taping drywall or wiring a fixture.

Of course, there's a point where planning becomes avoidance. However, you'll get itchy before then and want to go hammer something, so I'm not worried about over-planning.

Fortunately, you've taken the best first step: You've decided to get some guidance—this book. Thank you. As payback, I'll use this first part to guide you through the planning stages of finishing your basement. You'll figure out what you have, what you want, and how the heck you'll pay for it.

Let's start doodling!

In This Chapter

◆ Taking a look at your basement for more living space

◆ The pros and cons of basement remodeling

◆ Things you can do with your basement

◆ Figuring out whether you'll do it yourself, hire a contractor, or both

Expanding Your Home

There comes a point in every home's life when the walls become too close together. Children need their own play space. Teens want a party room. Parents need a quiet place to relax. Someone needs an office. Someone else wants a fitness center or hobby room. An in-law needs a place to live. Everyone needs extra living space!

Fortunately, more than a third of all homes in the United States have extra space available in the form of an unfinished basement. It could be little more than a crawlspace or it might be a partially finished basement that can quickly become rooms.

This chapter will open your mind up to the world of the basement and how it can be converted into valuable living space at a cost much lower than expanding your home horizontally. Even if you've already started thinking about remodeling your basement, this chapter can help you solidify your plans—and help you consider the best uses for your basement.

Let's go down to the basement. Watch your step!

Going Underground: All About Basements

Basements have been a vital part of homes for hundreds of years. In some parts of the United States they serve as shelter from the storm, or as a place to store food during the winter. In the western United States, partial basements are built under hillside houses to utilize the supporting foundation. In extreme climates the basement is where all the bulky heating and cooling equipment is installed. Many new homes include an unfinished basement as a "bonus area" for future expansion.

The primary reason why homeowners should first look down when expanding their homes is cost. The perimeter walls and typically the floor are already in place in an unfinished basement. The second reason is that the typical do-it-yourselfer can do the job without a contractor. The skills and tools you'll need are offered in this book.

Is It Worth It?

Real estate experts will tell you that finishing a basement is the most economical way to add living space to homes with "bonus" or unfinished space. Because the perimeter walls are built and the services are wired and plumbed in, the cost of finishing a basement is typically about *half* the cost of adding on to your home. Contact a local real estate appraiser for specific valuations in your neighborhood.

What Is a Basement?

A *basement* is the part of a building that is partly or completely below ground level. If it has rooms, especially ones for storing food, it's often called a *cellar*. If the area below the first floor isn't high enough for someone to stand under it's called a *crawlspace*. Some builders differentiate this below-grade space thus:

◆ If it has a solid floor and you can stand up, it's a basement.

◆ If it has a dirt floor and you can stand up, it's a cellar.

◆ If it has a dirt floor and you can't stand up, it's a crawlspace.

Deeper Meaning

A **basement** is the bottom story of a building below the first or ground floor. A basement may be partially or completely below surrounding grade. A **cellar** is a room or group of rooms below or predominantly below grade, usually under a building. A **crawlspace** is the area between the first floor and the ground sufficient for crawling, but not for standing. All of these terms are subject to regional definitions.

Other builders say that a basement is the below-grade space that can be accessed using interior stairs and a cellar is accessed using exterior stairs. For simplicity, this book will refer to any potential living space under the main floor of a residence as the basement.

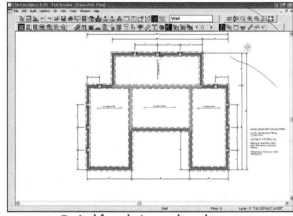

Typical foundation under a house.

Pros and Cons of Basement Living Spaces

Finishing a basement offers many advantages to homeowners who need extra space. Foremost, the space already is enclosed. Finishing it off is less expensive than building new space beside or above the existing foundation. In addition, services such as electricity, water, and heating, are nearby, typically in the main floor's flooring system (the basement's ceiling). Finally, most homeowners have or can easily develop the skills needed to finish a basement.

What's the downside to finishing your basement into living space? Finishing a basement that has structural or water problems can be more expensive than starting anew. Of course, they need to be taken care of anyway, so deciding to finish the basement gives you a good reason to repair it. Also, depending on the type of basement your home has (covered in the next section), it may be too small to be useful for anything but storage. Fortunately, you may be able to expand and finish a crawlspace or cellar into a partial or even full basement. This book will show you how.

On the Level

Consider remodeling the stairway to your basement. It really helps to open the side stair walls and provide a feeling that it's just another part of the house and not the basement.

Basement Types

There are many types of basements built under homes. So one of your first tasks will be to determine what type your home has. A *full basement* is approximately the same size and height as the home's main floor. A *partial basement* is one that is about 80 percent or less the size of the first or main floor. A *closed basement* can only be accessed from stairs on the home's main floor. A *walkout* or *daylight basement* is one that includes a door directly out from the basement.

Here are a few other basement terms: a *finished basement* is one that can be lived in; that is it has walls, electrical and plumbing service, and a finished floor. In most homes a finished basement is sectioned off into rooms, typically

each with a specific purpose: bedroom, bathroom, recreation room, laundry, storage, etc. An *unfinished basement* is one that isn't—but could—be finished. The purpose of this book is to help you turn an unfinished basement into a finished one.

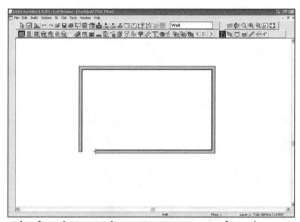

The foundation is the perimeter support for a house.

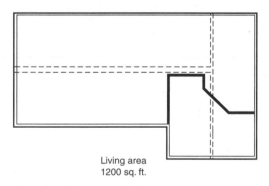

Living area
1200 sq. ft.

Some foundations include interior support walls.

A small bathroom can be installed to make your new basement more livable.

Your basement can house a laundry room and sink.

Basement Construction

Because the basement is at least partially below ground level, the walls must be strong and resistant to moisture. How strong and how resistant depends on the soil and water drainage around your home. In addition, the basement wall serves as the foundation for the above-ground floors in your home.

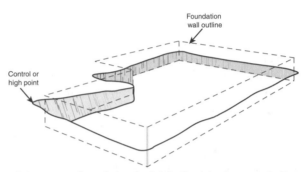

A basement foundation is dug before the house is built.

Homes without basements can be built on foundations that use pressure-treated wood. However, wood is porous and cannot easily be sealed to stop water from seeping around it so wood foundations typically aren't used for basement walls.

Poured *concrete* is popular as a foundation material, especially in houses with basements. A wide pad of concrete is poured well below grade to serve as a footing for the foundation walls. Because concrete is a liquid until it dries and hardens, temporary forms are used to hold the concrete in place. Reinforcement bar (called *rebar*) is placed in the forms to strengthen the concrete walls.

Deeper Meaning

Concrete is a mixture of aggregates and cement that hardens to a stonelike form and is used for foundations, paving, and many other construction purposes.

An alternate method of building foundation/basement walls is to make them out of concrete blocks or clay bricks atop a poured concrete footing. The rebars are inserted through vertical holes in the blocks or bricks to reinforce the walls.

Depending on local building codes and geology, a drainage system typically is installed on the outside of the foundation/basement wall to keep water away. In addition, the exterior surface is treated with waterproofing materials.

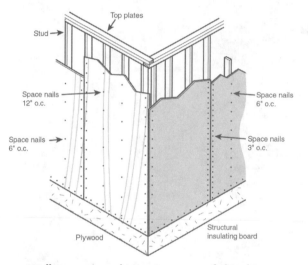

Walls are covered in moisture-proof sheathing.

Chapters 2 and 5 offer additional tips on waterproofing your basement. If you'd like to learn more about how new houses are constructed, read my book, *The Complete Idiot's Guide to Building Your Own Home* (Alpha Books, 2002) available from local bookstores or online at www.MulliganBooks.com.

Popular Basement Remodeling Ideas

As you can see, finishing your basement into valuable and attractive living space *can* be done. In fact, each year, many thousands of homeowners do it. To help you see the possibilities, let's take a look at some of the things people are doing with their basements:

- Root cellar for storing fruits and vegetables, and for growing mushrooms
- Wine cellar for storing wine and homemade beverages
- Pantry for storing sealed and canned foods
- Dry storage for seasonal clothing and unused household appliances
- Family room for playing games, reading, or watching television together
- Recreation or playroom for children's games and toys
- Fitness room for exercise equipment, sauna, spa, or hot tub
- Workshop for metalworking or woodworking
- Hobby room for trains, crafts, and other fun pastimes
- Laundry center for washing, drying, ironing, and mending clothes
- Den for relaxing around a fireplace
- Home office for working at home or paying the household bills

- Home theater for watching movies and listening to music
- Music room for practicing, jamming, and playing instruments or playing the stereo
- Kitchen for making a meal or a snack for basement inhabitants
- Bedroom for adults, children, in-laws, or guests
- Bathroom for everyone

- Teen or in-law apartment that combines two or more rooms for separate living
- Rental apartment that brings in income to help you pay for your new finished basement

Yes, there are many ways you can use that unfinished basement as welcome living space. Any room function in your home can be moved to the basement.

Your new basement can be turned into an English pub!

Your basement can be a single multipurpose room.

No space is wasted as this alcove is turned into a hideaway.

Make sure doors are wide enough to bring in major appliances.

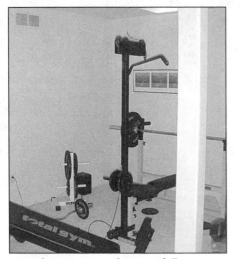

Your new basement can house a full gymnasium.

This kitchen is ideal for entertaining.

You can set up a desk for crafts, hobbies, a computer, or other fun activities.

Moving the laundry to the basement gives you more room upstairs.

A built-in ironing board can add functionality to your basement laundry room.

Imagine a fireplace like this in your new basement!

A divider wall can be installed to hide the toilet.

A small bath vanity in the basement reduces stair traffic.

A small apartment can be set up within the basement.

A small counter can serve as a dining area for a basement.

This wet bar serves as a kitchenette in a multipurpose basement room.

Home entertainment centers can turn your basement into a theater.

A small entertainment center can be set up in its own alcove within a multifunction room.

Larger kitchens are needed if the basement will be an apartment.

A kitchen can be installed on one wall of a basement room.

This finished basement includes a kitchenette, exercise equipment, and living space in a multipurpose room.

Creative Basement Ideas

To make your new basement unique, think of all the ways you can combine two or more rooms into practical living space. Apartments are good additions for those who have parents or siblings who need in-home care. A rental apartment can help ease the mortgage for a few years until it's time to evict the tenant so a teen or elderly parent can move in.

Some homeowners move main floor rooms to the basement to keep all the bedrooms on a single floor. So a home office is often the first candidate for the basement. Family rooms are popular, too, and can be multifunctional, serving as a play/fitness/game/computer/guest room.

If you're considering a home-based business, consider the basement as its home. If you will have customers or deliveries coming to the door you will need easy access for them. If your business is primarily by telephone and online, a basement offers both the space and the separation needed to become the home of a successful business.

You also can plan for the future, finishing off one end of the basement for current needs and making plans for additional rooms once your budget recuperates. Fortunately, an unfinished basement offers lots of creative options.

Who Does the Work?

Right about now you might be asking: Do I really want to do all the work necessary to transform a below-grade box into a practical living space? Am I up to this?

Construction Zone

Don't fall for the hucksters who go door-to-door selling remodeling services. Make sure you use a licensed and qualified contractor if you hire one to finish your basement. Also, if the contractor hires any employees, make sure all workers are covered by the contractor's worker's compensation insurance.

The answer is, you probably are! Fortunately, the skills needed for most basement remodeling jobs are teachable. You can learn how to install new walls, run electrical wiring, connect fixtures, plumb a bathroom or kitchen, install new flooring, paint, and finish your new living space. This book includes more than 300 photos and illustrations to show you how to tackle primary jobs. In addition, it offers suggestions for when and where to consider hiring outside help. You don't *have* to install your own

bathroom fixtures. But knowing how it's done will help you get your money's worth from experts you hire.

For most folks, there's more to being a do-it-yourselfer than acquired skills. It's the sense of pride that comes with doing it yourself. So what if the flooring isn't perfect or there are a few runs in the paint? It's yours. After all, it's the basement. Chances are, only your family and other friendly folk will ever see it.

Then there's the money issue. You may not be able to work as fast as a professional dry-waller, but you don't have to pay yourself $40 an hour either. If the choice is between a partially finished basement using contractors and a fully finished basement you remodel yourself, most homeowners will opt to do as much of the job themselves as possible.

That doesn't mean you shouldn't consider hiring one or more contractors. In fact, you might start by getting bids on the entire remodeling job, then decide which projects you want to do and which should be hired out.

I hope you're excited about the opportunities that lie ahead for finishing your home's basement. Just as important, I hope you're confident in your own ability to learn new things and test your skills. You can do this!

The Least You Need to Know

◆ Millions of homes include basements that can be used as extra living space for a variety of uses.

◆ Basement remodeling is a relatively inexpensive way to extend your home's functionality.

◆ It's important to repair any moisture problems in your basement before remodeling begins.

◆ You probably can do some or all of the work needed to remodel your basement.

In This Chapter

- ◆ Finding living space in your basement
- ◆ Figuring out how much space you have
- ◆ Making the basement habitable
- ◆ Solving some common basement problems

Chapter 2

Finding Space

Yes, unfinished basements are excellent candidates for finishing into attractive, livable space. But what about *your* home's basement? Is it big enough? Does it have enough headroom? What about the floor? How can you make sure it's dry enough?

These are a few of the important topics I'll cover in this chapter. In the following chapter you'll actually design your basement—and Chapter 4 will help you figure out how you're going to pay for it. But first, let's make sure that *your* home's basement is a qualified candidate for the work ahead.

About Living Space

What kind of space do you need for living? Of course, that's subjective. Some folks can do well with a small home while others require a triple car garage and a pole building out back for extra storage.

Finished basements often combine purposes in one or two rooms.

Fortunately, there are some standards for determining what is and isn't living space. Counties and cities have published *building codes* that define habitable living space. These codes are standardized across the United States with only small changes locally. The definition of habitable space typically doesn't change from place to place. There are minimum size, height, and other requirements to call a space "livable."

> **Deeper Meaning**
>
> **Building codes** are a collection of legal requirements for the construction of buildings.

Minimum Size

Most building codes say that a room must be at least 7 feet wide and be 70 square feet in size to be habitable. Of course, that doesn't mean

you can't have storage areas that are smaller. It just means that if you intend to have people use it as living space it must be at least that size to pass building code.

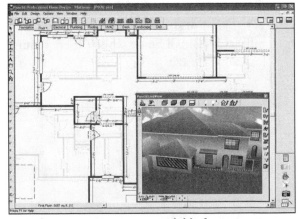

Software programs are available for estimating living space and requirements.

In addition, bedrooms, kitchens, and bathrooms typically have specific size requirements dictated by local building codes. You'll find that building codes in rural areas are less stringent than those in cities.

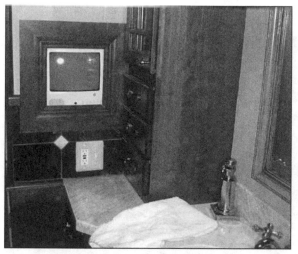

To save space, a built-in TV can be designed into a high-traffic room.

Here's a creative way to use otherwise wasted space: a built-in bookcase.

Minimum Height

Building codes typically require that the height of a room (floor to ceiling) must be at least 7 feet 6 inches for the room to be considered habitable. An exception is made under most building codes for trusses or beams under the main floor (the basement's ceiling). If the beams are at least 4 feet apart the space below them can be 7 feet.

 **On the Level**

> Heavy-duty floor trusses require less support from underneath so they require fewer posts. Their depth also gives you more room to install heating ducts, plumbing, and wiring between floors.

Most building codes also allow less height for a kitchen, bathroom, hallway, and sometimes other rooms. The limit for these typically is 7 feet.

This built-in bookcase swings out and opens to an unfinished storage area/crawlspace.

What about rooms where the height is not consistent? Most building codes allow lowered ceilings if at least half of the room meets the minimum requirements.

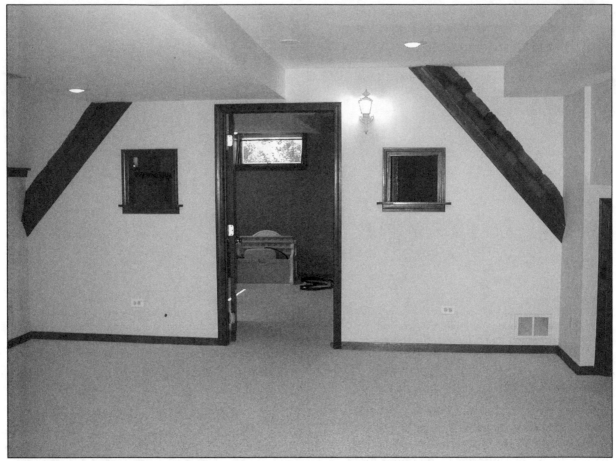

A room with an uneven ceiling can become a child's playroom.

Remember that these minimums are for *habitable* space. The space under a stairway, for example, won't fit the size or height minimums—so no one can live under the stairs. However, it is still usable space that can become storage. Also, bathrooms are not considered living space—no matter how long one spends in them. Laundry rooms, too, are not considered habitable.

Other Minimums

Building codes also require that hallways be at least 36 inches wide. There will be additional building code requirements. Codes and permits are covered more extensively in Chapter 5.

In and Out

Another requirement of living in your finished basement is being able to get in and out—called ingress and egress. Entrances and exits are specified in building code requirements, primarily for basement bedrooms because people sleeping there need an emergency exit in case of fire.

Building codes say a basement bedroom must have an exit, usually a window, with an opening of no less than 5 square feet and a minimum width of 24 inches. In addition, the lowest edge of the window must be no more than 44 inches from the floor. Those are the minimums. Practicality dictates that the bottom edge of bedroom windows for small children are even closer to the floor.

A closet for extra storage is behind this false wall.

Full stairway makes access easy.

Typical basement window for light only.

This bedroom window also serves as an emergency exit in a bedroom.

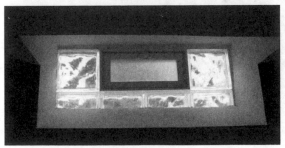

This basement window includes an opening pane to allow ventilation.

Basement bedrooms require an emergency exit through a window.

Posts and Support

Unfinished basements typically have *posts* and other supports that hold up the house's main floor. These posts are installed where required, not necessarily where they are most efficient for installing walls.

Deeper Meaning _____

A **post** is a vertical support member, usually made up of only one piece of lumber or a metal pipe or I-beam.

For example, your home's main floor has numerous walls, some of them are designed to hold up the roof or upper floors and others are simply room separators. The bearing walls are built to serve both as support and as separators. The bearing posts in the basement, however, are installed to support only.

That means your basement may have posts smack dab in the middle of a room you're planning. They will become a challenge in designing and finishing your basement. You can either move them or work around them; both options are covered in Chapter 6 on structural remodeling. As you seek and visualize living space in your home's basement, be aware of existing posts because they impact your living space.

This support post is less obtrusive because it is adjacent to a large object.

Posts can be disguised or objects can be placed at their base to reduce the chances of someone running into them.

Enclosing an area of support posts under stairs can turn the space into an alcove or storage.

Measuring Your Basement

As you can see, there's a lot of potential living space in an unfinished basement! How much space exactly? Let's find out. Grab some paper, a pencil, and a tape measure (25-foot is best).

Width and Length

The first measurement you want is the length of all space under your main floor whether it currently has access or not. (I'll cover estimating inaccessible space in a moment.) Because many unfinished basements aren't square, you may need to get the lengths at various locations.

Next, measure and record the widths. Even if your basement seems to be a single width, measure it in numerous locations and you may find that it varies slightly.

Calculating Square Feet

A square foot is an area 1 foot long by 1 foot wide. That's easy. However, calculating square feet of an basement area can be more difficult. It's easy to calculate the square footage of a basement that's 20 by 24 feet (480 square feet), but what do you do if your basement varies in width and length? You break the space up into squares and rectangles, calculate the square footage of each area, then add them all up. For initial planning, an approximate square footage is sufficient. However, as you start finishing your basement you'll want exact measurements and size.

Height

Earlier in this chapter, I covered the height requirements of habitable space. In some cases you'll need to calculate the total space in cubic feet. A cubic foot is an area 1 foot long by 1 foot wide by 1 foot high or deep. It's 1 square foot in the third dimension. A cubic foot is 1,729 cubic inches. A cubic yard ($3 \times 3 \times 3$) is 27 cubic feet. Some building contractors and suppliers estimate cost of materials and construction based on cubic feet. Also, cubic content is used when estimating the cost of installing heating, lighting, and ventilation systems.

Estimating Areas Without Access

How can you calculate the square or cubic footage of an area that you can't get to such as in an adjacent crawlspace? By estimating.

If you have access to the outside of the space, such as the house's perimeter, measure it. If possible, insert a broomstick or other object of known length into the space and use it to estimate widths and lengths. Or you may be able to feed a metal measuring tape into the area to get approximate dimensions.

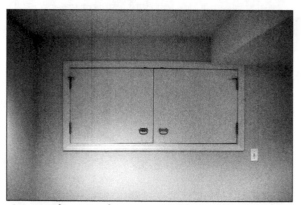

Areas without stand-up access can be used for storage.

Fortunately, because you won't be using these areas for living space you don't need exact dimensions. However, knowing their approximate size can help in planning.

Overcoming Basement Problems

Most unfinished basements have "issues" or problems that need to be solved to finish them and make them livable. It may be that the floor is partially or fully dirt. Or there are water stains on the walls indicating possible seepage—or maybe even standing water on the floor. Or there are pests that need to be eliminated before you can even begin to enter the basement.

Plumbing can be hidden behind built-ins as long as they have an access door.

Fortunately, the coming chapters will help you solve common basement problems. Alternately, you can call on contractors, exterminators, and cleaning services to help you get your basement ready for finishing. So here I'll cover three of the primary problems that require solutions before a basement can be finished: floors, moisture control, and drainage.

Floors

Most unfinished basements already have some type of solid and level flooring in place, even if it's just a concrete slab. Alternately, some basement floors are made of wood framing covered with wooden boards or plywood called a subfloor. However, you may find that the basement area you want to finish is little more than a dirt-floored crawlspace. What can you do?

First, ask how much height or headroom the basement currently has. Why? Because you want to make sure that, after adding a new 4-inch thick floor you have 7 feet 6 inches of height to make it livable (according to the building code). If the area can't be made livable, maybe it can be made useful for storage.

If your basement has sufficient height for installing a new floor over dirt you'll probably need to hire a contractor to install it. In fact, you may first need an excavation contractor to remove and level dirt, extracting it through a basement window or a new opening in the foundation. Then a framing or concrete contractor can prepare and install the new floor. If your basement has posts and supports, you'll probably need an engineer to help design the new floor.

Having given you the worst-case scenario, I'll tell you that dirt-floored, full-height basements are relatively rare and typically are found only under older rural homes. Most full-basement homes with concrete foundations also have reinforced concrete floors. And even the ones that don't can be retrofitted with a solid floor for less money than expanding your home horizontally.

On the Level

Often, concrete basement floors have cracks. Fortunately, they can be repaired either by the homeowner (using concrete repair products available at larger building material stores) or by concrete contractors. Make sure it gets done before installing your new flooring.

Moisture

Moisture is a house's enemy. Standing water on a floor, running down a wall, or dripping from a ceiling is a red flag that says, "Hey, we have a problem here!" Unfortunately, "here" isn't always where the problem started. Water from a roof leak can first show up a great distance from the entry point. A gutter's broken downspout can dump water along a basement wall instead of carrying it away from the building. A leaky pipe under the floor can carry water many feet before it finally drops off onto the basement floor. Or a crack in the concrete floor can allow water to seep up from the ground and puddle.

So, of course, you want to know if your basement is dry before finishing it off. Is that wet spot condensation from moisture in the room or is it seeping through a wall or floor? To find out, simply tape a 1-foot square piece of cellophane or aluminum foil tightly against the concrete wall and another against the concrete floor in various locations around the basement. Come back in 24 hours and touch the outside surface. If it's wet, the cause is condensation in the room. Then peel back the cover and look for moisture underneath. If moist or wet, the cause is seepage; water is somehow getting through.

How does water seep through a concrete floor or wall? Easily! Concrete is porous and the only way to stop seepage is by sealing the concrete. It's best to seal the concrete on the exterior so that it never enters the foundation or floor. However, if the foundation is already in place and backfilled (dirt is pushed up against it), it may be difficult to excavate and seal the foundation. The second option is to seal the concrete on the inside of the home. That means putting up a vapor or moisture barrier (usually some type of plastic sheeting) that keeps water out.

I'll cover interior waterproofing in Chapter 6 on structural remodeling.

Drainage

Most homes are built with some type of ground contouring or drainage system in place to keep moisture away from the foundation. However, time moves on—and rain moves dirt and gravel used for drainage. So, before you know it, water is running down the exterior, and ultimately the interior, basement walls.

The first solution is to check drainage around your home's foundation at least once a year and repair any little problems before they become big ones. You don't have to wait until winter. You can turn on a garden hose in the late spring, moving it to various points around the foundation to watch how the water runs and if it shows up where it shouldn't. If a problem is found you can get it repaired over the summer or fall before the rains set in. (Make appropriate adjustments to this plan if you live where rains fall in the summer rather than in the winter.)

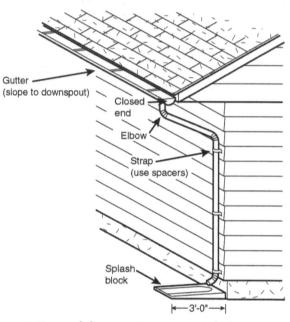

Gutters and downspouts serve as a drainage system for water running off the roof.

In many cases, the culprit is a clogged gutter that allows water to run over the edge and fall to within inches of the basement walls. The solution, of course, is to clean or repair the gutters.

You can solve minor drainage problems by clearing earth away from the foundation and installing drain gravel or pipe that encourages the water to flow away from the foundation rather than toward it. You can't really stop water from falling around a foundation; you just don't want it to linger.

If these solutions *still* don't solve the basement moisture problem, you'll have to dig deeper. You'll need to excavate around the foundation and install a vapor barrier to keep moisture off the concrete. Additionally, you can install a drain system at the foundation footing to move water away from the concrete.

What about a concrete floor that shows moisture seepage? If you've found no other way of sealing the floor, you may have to remove part of the floor (consider renting a hydraulic jackhammer or a strong young man) and install drainage pipe and/or gravel. This is typically not a job that most homeowners try to tackle themselves. However, you can cut contractor costs by doing some of the work, such as breaking up concrete as directed.

Deeper Meaning

A *sump pump* collects ground water from drain tile under a basement floor and exterior drain systems, and discharges it away from the house. To keep your basement's sump pump from overworking, make sure gutters and downspouts work well.

You may have heard or even seen a *sump pump* in a basement. A sump is a lined hole in the floor that catches moisture. A sump pump removes the moisture through an outside drain. If your basement already has a sump

pump, make sure it remains in good working condition. If your basement doesn't have one, but does collect moisture on the floor, consider installing one. A sump pump can be purchased as a unit in larger building material stores and installed by cutting a hole at the lowest point on the floor. Make sure electricity is nearby to power the pump. The unit will either include a pit liner or instructions for sealing the pit as well as specify its size.

A sump pump can be covered.

Getting eager to design your new basement? Me, too. That's the next topic. See you at Chapter 3!

The Least You Need to Know

◆ Building codes specify minimum room sizes and heights for habitable areas.

◆ Basement bedrooms require an emergency exit of a specific size and location.

◆ Carefully measure your unfinished basement to determine available space and to prepare for estimating costs.

◆ Below-ground basements may have moisture and other problems, but most can be solved.

In This Chapter

◆ Determining what function(s) your new basement will serve

◆ Making preliminary plans—and the many changes that often entails

◆ Finalizing your new basement plans

◆ Visualizing your finished basement with the help of software programs

Chapter 3

Designing Your Space

Your basement is like a blank piece of paper. You've determined how much useable space your basement has and you've considered some of the ways you could bring that space to life. Now it's time to start brainstorming and doodling, looking at all the ways you can get what you want from what you have. Finally, you'll decide what works best and how you'll get it done.

That's what this chapter is all about: planning. It isn't wasted effort. Every hour of smart planning can save a day of installing and removing real walls and doors. I'll first show you how to make function lists, then turn them into rough plans. You'll also learn how to sketch your new basement on paper or using some really neat computer software programs that can make you think you're already in your basement. Let's get started!

Functions and Requirements

It's easy to skim over the planning stage of any project, especially when you'd love to have it done yesterday. However, you'll begin enjoying your new basement faster—and longer—if you take a little time right now to consider the various functions your basement should have and list the requirements.

Listing Functions

A function is a purpose or characteristic. The function of a bedroom, for example, is to provide a comfortable and safe place to sleep and to dress. It also serves as a storage site for clothing, bedding, and related items. That makes sense. However, as you plan your basement, rooms may have more than one function. In fact, they may have multiple functions that you wouldn't normally consider.

Try to visualize how your finished basement might look.

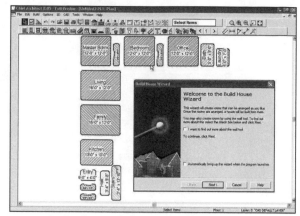

Think of your design as blocks of function.

A well-designed basement plan will include storage.

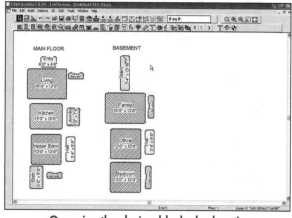

Organize the design blocks by location.

For example, a bedroom by night may be an office by day. A family room may double as a guest room. A bathroom may double as a utility or storage room if space is available. So a good place to start planning your new basement is to list the various functions you want it to serve as a whole. You can then match up related functions into specific rooms.

The size and available space in your unfinished basement will limit the functions that it can serve. For now, though, list all the functions you want in the space. Your list may look like this:

◆ Permanent sleeping for older children

◆ Area for entertaining including a kitchenette and small bathroom

◆ Somewhere to store all those holiday decorations

◆ An area to set up a small desk for a game system

◆ Somewhere comfortable for watching movies

◆ An in-law apartment for elderly parents

◆ A place to get away from it all

You get the picture. Start a list of such functions, reviewing the various functions that people put basements to (see Chapter 1). Make sure others in your living group get the opportunity to add to the list, too, even young children; for example:

◆ A place to play with my dolls
◆ Somewhere I can play my new guitar without my sister bothering me

These functions may or may not make the final cut—or they may be combined with related functions—but they will provide a sense of ownership that can make cooperation and cleanup easier. (Hey, it's worth a try!)

Determining Requirements

Hopefully, your function list is long and includes both must-haves and gee-that-would-be-nices. Next comes figuring out what each function's requirements will be. It sounds simple, but it's really important to think these elements through before finalizing basement plans and spending time and money making them happen.

For example, the function of a needed bathroom may include a shower, bathtub, sink, toilet, bidet, or other components depending on its function. Is the bathroom for young people or for the elderly who will be living in basement bedrooms? The requirements are different. Young people may want only a shower, or they will shower in an upstairs bathroom. Older people may need a bathtub with easy access.

Think, too, about future requirements. Eventually, the bathroom may need access for elderly or disabled people. Or the basement may be designed to become a rental apartment once the last kid goes off to college.

Then there are the physical or building code requirements. For example, a below-ground-level bathroom may require special plumbing or bathroom fixtures. You also can add the required size of a room, such as 10 feet by 12 feet for a children's bedroom. In addition, local building codes probably will require an emergency exit for bedrooms. If your basement doesn't have an easy egress through an outside wall it may be very expensive to include a bedroom in your design because of code requirements.

Built-in cabinets and drawers can utilize otherwise wasted space.

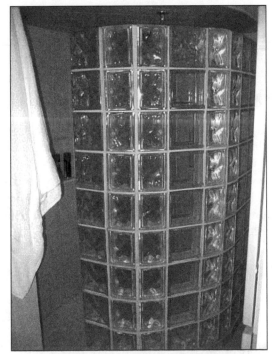

A glass wall can allow light into an otherwise dark basement space.

Special-use rooms also will have special requirements. For example, an office probably will require a telephone line and possibly network wiring for a computer. A home theater will require wiring for the audio and video components as well as some soundproofing.

On the Level

Egress or an escape route is required in basements with bedrooms. Remodelers suggest that you install composite window wells that have built-in ladders on the exterior. If you're installing a standard window, use frosted glass to allow light in without viewing the well.

The point here is to list not only the functions you want the basement space to serve, but also the requirements of these functions. As you actually plan the layout of your finished basement, you'll see how this list can help you decide what should be in it. Even if you choose to hire an architect to draw the final plans, you'll be ahead in the process—and *save money*—by thinking in terms of functions and requirements.

Making Rough Plans

What's next? Matching up the functional needs with the physical space. Actually, this part is kind of fun. It may seem like putting 5 pounds of potatoes in a 3-pound bag, but it offers the opportunity for creative space design. You may find that your new basement can include more functionality than you thought possible. Let's give it a try.

Sketching by Function

It doesn't matter whether you're an artist or not, you can start drawing plans for your new finished basement. That's because you'll start with circles. Simply draw circles on a sheet of paper and include in them related functions. For example, one circle may include the functions of a family

room. Another may be a game room. Another circle from your function list may include a bathroom. Another may be a laundry room. Lots of circles, each with a specific function.

Now what? Draw lines between these circles to show any relationships. That is, a bedroom needs a nearby bathroom. A kitchen serves the family room or recreation room. A home theater doesn't require other rooms so it stands alone in a circle. These are rooms that need each other.

Finally, use a different color pencil to draw lines between circles of similar use. That is, a daytime office space also can serve as a home entertainment space during the evening and on weekends. A children's play space could serve double duty as a hobby space. Remember, these aren't rooms yet, just functional spaces.

If you have a computer you can use one of various software programs to do these functional sketches (covered later in this chapter). Because these are just circles and lines, any simple drawing program found on many computers, such as Corel Draw or Microsoft Visio, will serve the purpose for now. You're attempting to help visualize the relationship of functional spaces. Use whatever tool, pencil or computer, that makes it easy.

Sizing Functions

The next task in planning is to estimate how much space you'll need for each of these functional areas or circles. For example, by measuring an existing bedroom in your home you may determine that a new basement bedroom will require 120 square feet to be practical. Or you may need at least an 8-feet-by-10-feet (80 square feet) space for your home office. Write these numbers down in the appropriate circles on your functional plan.

Then total it all up. Your functional plan and wish list may include seven functional areas that require 800 square feet or more of space. If the unfinished basement area measures 800 square feet the final decisions are easier. If, however, the functional areas you want don't match the available space, you have some more planning to do. Fortunately, all the circles and lines you just drew will make trimming much easier.

In the real world, you may come up with two or three different functional plans. That's okay. The process is about considering all options and requirements, then whittling them down to the best. Remember: Paper planning is *much* cheaper than construction changes!

Drawing Finished Plans

Finished plans with all the specific details of construction are *vital* to your basement project. If the project requires a building permit (most do) you'll need to file construction drawings with the local building department. If you're after financing, your lender probably will require a set of plans. If you're using a contractor or subcontractor for some or all of the work, again, you'll need plans.

Not a Computer Nut?

Not everyone has—or even wants—a computer. If you'd prefer to draw out your own plans, stop by your local stationery store for graph paper, mechanical pencils, and rulers. You can use each quarter-inch square of the graph paper to represent 1 foot of your basement, meaning a 20-feet-by-30-feet basement will be 5 inches by 6 inches on paper.

What plans? Some of the various drawn plans used in construction include these:

◆ *Site plan*

◆ Foundation plan

◆ Interior and exterior elevations (representational drawings of interior and exterior walls to show finish features)

◆ Floor plan

Deeper Meaning

A **site plan** is a drawing of all the existing conditions on the lot, usually including slope and other topography, existing utilities, and setbacks. You may be able to get a copy of your home's site plan from the local municipality.

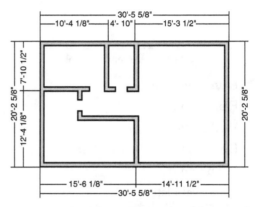

You can use a software program to draw and even size your unfinished basement.

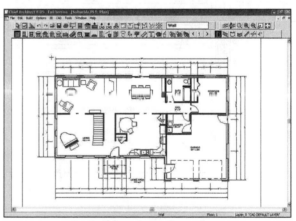

Typical basement floor plan including furniture placement.

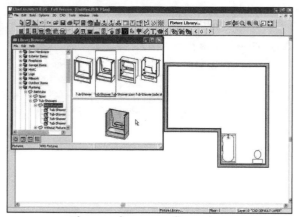

Alternate basement floor plan.

◆ Plumbing plan

◆ Framing plan

◆ Wall section

◆ Door and window schedule

◆ Plumbing plan

◆ Electrical plan

◆ Room finish schedule

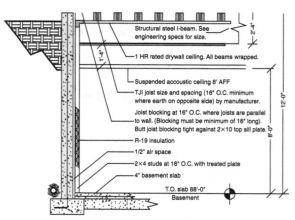

Basement wall section.

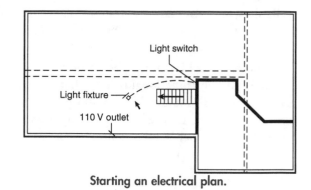

Starting an electrical plan.

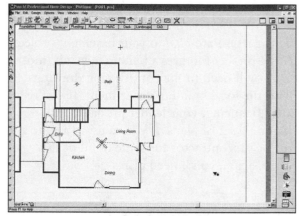

Expanded electrical plan.

Chapter 5 covers the required plans and permits in more detail. It also describes specification sheets and materials lists that you'll need for finishing your basement.

On the Level

Should you use an architect to help you design and finish your basement? Of course, that depends on your skills and your budget. An architect typically charges about 15 to 25 percent of the project's value for his or her services. The higher percentage is for projects where the architect also serves as a remodeling manager or general contractor.

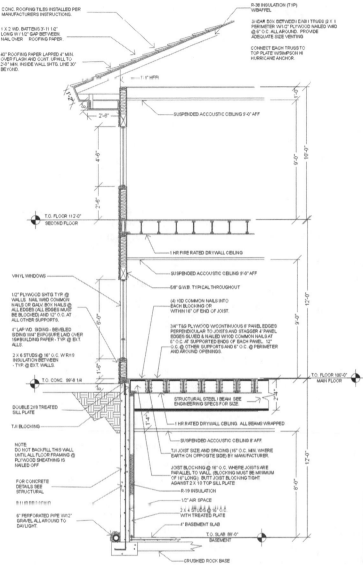

TYPICAL SECTION
1/2" = 1-0"

Typical construction section.

Making Plans

Where will all these plans come from? If you're using a contractor, he or she can provide the final plans. The same goes for an architect. But what if you're doing it all (or at least most of it) yourself? You can hire a drafting service to draw up required plans from your rough plan. Or you can draw them yourself using one of the popular software tools.

Using Design and Plan Software

The computer has revolutionized many industries, not the least of which is construction and remodeling. Professionals have powerful tools for sketching, sizing, placing, and designing everything from small rooms to housing complexes. Fortunately for consumers, many of these powerful (and expensive) tools have consumer-level counterparts that are inexpensive (under $100) and quite useful in designing and planning projects like finishing basements.

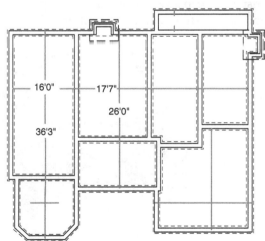

Calculating room dimensions with a software program.

Professional Home Design (PHD), distributed by Punch Software (www.punchsoftware.com), is a popular home construction and remodeling design program that is actually a family of programs. PHD allows you to start a design by quickly drawing the perimeter of the foundation, then adding the flooring system, electrical, plumbing, roofing, HVAC (heating, ventilation, and air conditioning), and even landscaping. You can draw your existing home then add a basement under it so you get the big picture, or you can simply draw a floor and set the working elevation as a minus number (below grade) to indicate that it is a basement. Once you've placed all the walls, doors, and other components, it can produce electrical, plumbing, and HVAC plans for your printer in seconds. PHD and many other consumer design programs also can develop and print materials lists for projects. You can use these lists to get bids from suppliers.

However, one of the most popular components of this and other home design and remodeling software packages is the 3-dimensional or 3-D view. Once your plan is completed you can virtually walk through your new basement on the computer screen, turning left or right as needed. In addition, many of these programs can instantly strip away the surfaces to expose floor joists, wall studs, and ceiling rafters.

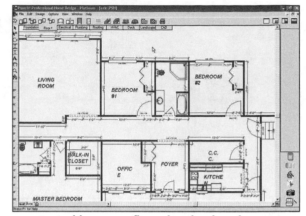

Typical basement floor plan developed using Professional Home Design.

Construction Zone

Make sure the remodeling and design software you select is appropriate to your needs. Don't purchase one that will take weeks to learn and even more time to use. If you have Internet access, download trial copies of various design programs to determine which is best for your needs.

Other consumer home design software includes myHouse from DesignSoft (www.designsoftware.com), Classic Home Design from Artifice (www.artifice.com), SmartDraw (www.smartdraw.com), and 3D Home Architect developed by Advanced Relational Technology and distributed by Broderbund Software (www.broderbund.com).

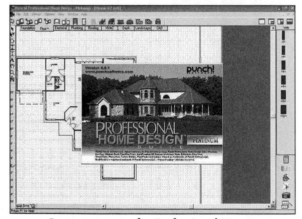

Computer screen for Professional Home Design from Punch Software.

On the higher end are products such as Chief Architect, also from Advanced Relational Technology (ART) and sold direct (www.chiefarchitect.com). Developed for architects, builders, designers, and drafters, it's more expensive than consumer design products. Then again, you get what you pay for. The library that comes with it includes 7,000 symbols, textures, and images to make a walk-through almost feel like you've broken into someone's home. You can even specify a door or window by manufacturer and size, for example, and plop it in to your design to see what it will look like. Once you're done you can have the program print out a one-dimension model that can be cut and assembled into a three-dimensional room or house. Talk about seeing what you're getting into!

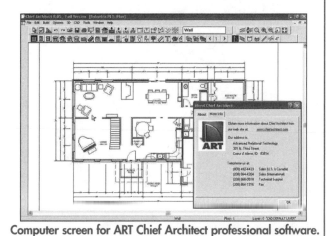

Computer screen for ART Chief Architect professional software.

Three-dimensional house plan.

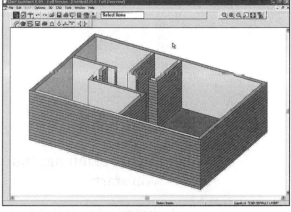

Three-dimensional foundation plan.

There are numerous other features available in consumer- and pro-level home remodeling design software. And there are many other software programs available as well. Larger computer software stores will have a few on hand. Otherwise, check online, download trial versions, and have some fun designing your new basement.

The Least You Need to Know

- ◆ The first step to an efficient basement design is determining its various functions.
- ◆ Make a sketch of the requirements, including space, needed for each function in your new basement.
- ◆ Your basement remodeling project will need comprehensive plans and drawings to meet building and financing requirements.
- ◆ Various popular software programs can make designing, planning, documenting, and visualizing your finished basement easier.

In This Chapter

- ◆ Smart planning: four questions to ask yourself before you start

- ◆ Estimating what it will cost to finish your basement

- ◆ Finding ways to pay for basement remodeling

- ◆ Can you live with the mess?

Chapter 4

Budgeting Your Project

Wouldn't it be great if rich Uncle Bud said, "Hey, finish your basement. I'll pay the bill!" In your dreams!

The first reality of basement remodeling is that it will cost more than you thought. The second reality is that *you*, not the state lottery nor an eccentric uncle, will pay for the project. Sure, you can finance some or all of it over the rest of whatever, but it's still *your money*—plus interest!

This chapter is for those without rich uncles. It shows you how to estimate costs, cut them, and find the least expensive financing, if needed. It also offers some options you may not have considered. This chapter, above all, can save you thousands of basement remodeling dollars—and help you survive the project.

Smart Planning

Is finishing your basement really a good idea? Or will you wind up with a partially finished basement and no money to pay the mortgage?

There are thousands of partially finished basements in the United States and Canada. Some are the victims of lost jobs or domestic changes, but many are not finished because the owners weren't sure of what they were getting in to. They didn't think it through, figuring costs and finding ways to keep them within their means. That won't happen to you because you're doing it right, planning the job before you smack the first nail.

On the Level

> Suppose one of you wants to build a tower [or a basement]. Will he not first sit down and estimate the cost to see if he has enough money to complete it? For if he lays the foundation and is not able to finish it, everyone who sees it will ridicule him, saying, "This fellow began to build and was not able to finish."
>
> —Luke 14:28–30 New International Version

Before I even get into estimating costs, though, here are four questions you should answer. As they are asked I'll expand on them to help you answer to the best of your knowledge. Your answers are important to determining the total cost and value of your new basement.

How Long Will You Live Here?

It's impossible for most folks to know exactly how long they will live in a specific home before moving on. Jobs change. Life makes unplanned announcements. Other investments ripen or go sour, altering finances. However, what's your best current estimation of how long you expect to live in your current home?

The answer is important because basement remodeling is a long-term project, typically taking a few months to a year. In addition, you may not get all of your investment back if you must sell your home with a partially finished basement. In areas where home values appreciate fast, finishing a basement can be an excellent investment that multiplies potential profits from the sale of your home. In places where home values increase slowly—or actually go down—some of the money spent on finishing a basement may be lost until the home appreciates more in value.

Is It an Expense or an Investment?

Your answer to the second question, expense or investment, depends on what you're doing with the basement. If you're adding a family room or a home theater, it's an expense and no financial payback is expected. However, if you're installing a home office for you or production space for your small home-based business, it's an investment. It's also an investment if you're installing an income-producing apartment. Maybe you'll be renting it out to strangers or maybe elderly parents moving in to the basement apartment have agreed to help out with construction costs or pay a small rental fee. In any case, it's an investment.

Finishing a basement means planning for walls, windows, floors, lighting, trim—and how to pay for it all.

As an investment, all or part of your basement can be treated as income-producing property. That is, the expenses might be written off your income tax obligation or qualify for a higher mortgage amount because of the income that it will bring in. If you're getting into areas of taxation, spend a few bucks to talk with a tax accountant with small business or real estate investment experience.

How Much Could It Cost?

Again, I'll get into estimating actual construction costs in a moment. For now, consider how much finishing your basement *could* cost, a ballpark number.

How? By developing a per-square-foot cost based on the value of the remainder of your home. An example works well here. If you have a 2,000-square-feet home worth $200,000 (not counting the land), the per-square-foot valuation is $100. Figuring that about two thirds of that value is in the structural skeleton and one third in the finishing, the value of finishing is about $35 per square foot. Apply this valuation against the example basement size of, say, 800 square feet and you come up with a ballpark estimate of $28,000.

Obviously, this is a broad ballpark. However, it serves as an initial reality check. Is this a realistic number for you? Were you thinking more like about half this amount or double it? It's an important question because it may tell you to consider finishing *part* of your basement now and the remainder later—when Uncle Bud leaves his fortune to you. Even if it does seem like more than you can spend, don't give up yet. Keep reading to find ways of cutting—and financing—costs that you may not have considered.

How Will You Pay for It?

It doesn't look like Uncle Bud will come through with a blank check, so how *will* you pay for finishing your basement? The section "Funding Your Basement Remodel," later in this chapter, will offer specifics. For now, consider your options: cash (savings, cashing out investments, pay-as-you-go, lottery winnings), consumer loans, or a new first or second mortgage. These are your primary options. Those who rent money from others have the additional cost of interest paid. Those who take assets from other investments (savings) lose the potential interest earned on what they withdraw.

Estimating Costs

Answering the previous four questions serves as a reality check for how long you plan to use the basement, whether it's an investment or an expense, how much it could cost, and how you might pay for it. It's now time to get out of the ballpark and get specific. You need to know more accurately what it will cost for finishing your basement.

Worksheets from Plans

If you're using one of the computer software programs as described in Chapter 3, you may already have the tools you need to develop an accurate cost estimate. Many of them, especially the higher-priced programs, include a materials worksheet that lists the materials needed for your basement remodel. Depending on the software, you can print out the materials list and visit suppliers for actual costs, or print it and give it to suppliers for their bid, or use online suppliers or resources to fill in the costs.

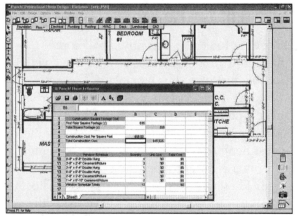

Design software programs typically include a materials estimator function.

Getting Bids

Whether or not you're using a remodeling or design program, you can take the printed plans to building material suppliers and ask them to bid on materials. It's easier for them—and more accurate for you—if you can supply a specific materials list, but most suppliers can work directly from your remodel plans as long as the plans are comprehensive.

Spreadsheets

Depending on the complexity of your basement remodeling project and your comfort level with computer software, you can develop a spreadsheet to help you in estimating materials and costs. The first column is for specific materials and subsequent columns are for costs from various suppliers. Or you can put materials in the first column with sizes and prices in the other columns. The advantage to a spreadsheet program is that it quickly can do the math for you.

Alternatively, you can buy some columnar accounting pads from a stationery store and fill in the blanks with your calculator nearby.

Funding Your Basement Remodel

The question was asked earlier in this chapter: How will you pay for finishing your basement? Various options were mentioned. Let's consider each option in more detail because each has additional costs whether in interest paid or interest lost.

Some homeowners fund their basement project in stages, first finishing then furnishing.

Cash

Cash is good. In fact, if you can pay for your basement remodeling project in cash you typically can earn a small discount from most suppliers. The discount can range from 2 to 10 percent of the total. To get the discount, speak with the manager of various material suppliers in your area to find out who has the best *net* (after discounts) prices for cash transactions.

Remember that even if you are borrowing the money to finance the job, a supplier that receives payment within 10 days of the purchase probably will give you a same-as-cash discount.

Some folks with smaller basement remodeling projects use cash on a pay-as-you-go basis. That is, they set aside a specific amount each month from savings, regular income, or a combination of both, and buy what they need once a month. They then install it over the coming month. The remodel is then paid for by the time the work is done. No interest.

Consumer Loans

You can get a consumer loan for what you need either through a consumer loan company or on your credit card. The problem here is the higher interest rate. If you don't pay the loan off, the lender comes after you, not your house and new basement. From the lender's standpoint there is less security for the loan, your promise to pay. That's why the lender gets the higher interest.

However, for smaller remodeling projects that you plan to pay off in just a few months, a consumer loan or credit card purchase is typically easier to get than refinancing your house.

Mortgages

A *mortgage* is a loan that uses real estate as security. If you don't pay, the lender comes and takes your house. Because the security typically is worth more than the loan amount, the lender's risk is reduced. That means the interest rate charged is lower than the rate of higher-risk consumer loans.

> **Deeper Meaning** _____
>
> A **mortgage** is an agreement between a lender and a buyer using real property as security for the loan.

The primary mortgage against your home, the one you probably signed when you bought your house, is called the first mortgage. If you want to use some of the equity in your home as collateral for your basement remodel you can refinance your first mortgage *or* get a second mortgage.

What's the difference? You'll be paying off both mortgages simultaneously. It's just that if you default on your mortgages, the lender that holds your first mortgage gets paid off first. So interest rates on a second mortgage may be slightly higher than on the first because of the lender's higher risk.

The good news is that the increased value of your home with a newly finished basement typically can be the equity you need to fund it. Should you refinance your first mortgage, get a second mortgage, or go for a shorter-term home-equity loan? Good question! The answer depends on the equity you now have in your home, the value of your remodel, how much you need to get the job done, and current mortgage rates. You can start your search for the best answer by talking with your current mortgage lender.

Inspections and Draws

If your remodel project is small and you are self-financed (cash, consumer loan, or credit card) you won't have a mortgage. With a mortgage often comes lender requirements such as inspections. If, for example, you have a $20,000 second mortgage to finance finishing your basement, the lender probably will define specific points at which money will be paid to you, a supplier, and/or a contractor. The lender probably won't put all $20,000 in your checking account and let you spend it on a new car. Its purpose is to increase the value or equity you have in your home.

> **On the Level** _____
>
> Want to hire the best contractor in town? You can't! He's too busy. However, busy contractors often will recommend other contractors that they know are qualified but not as busy. So start at the top when looking for a basement remodeling contractor.

Inspections may be set for when all walls are framed, then once the plumbing and electrical systems are installed, and finally once the basement is finished and habitable. The lender may release chunks of money at each step, called *draw requests*. The challenge for you and/or your contractor is to make sure the draws cover the expenses to that point. If the framing draw is $5,000 and the framing contractor's bill is $8,000, for example, someone (guess who) will need to come up with $3,000 to pay the contractor. If you're working with a general contractor who is managing the project, he or she will coordinate the work and the draws. If you're doing it yourself, you'll need to coordinate them.

Deeper Meaning _____

A **draw request** is a monthly request by a contractor or do-it-yourself home-owner to be paid for the materials and labor installed into the project during the previous 30 days, to be drawn from the construction loan.

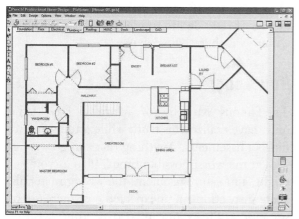

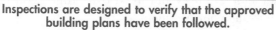

Inspections are designed to verify that the approved building plans have been followed.

The finished plumbing must meet local building codes and the approved building plans.

About Liens

A lien is legal charge against a project. A mechanic's lien is one made by a contractor, and a materials lien is made by someone who supplies materials for the job. Liens tell every-one "I have done some of the work or supplied some of the material for this job and I won't release my rights to get paid until I actually do get paid."

Lenders who make payments to contractors and suppliers will require that they simultane-ously sign off on the lien saying that it has been satisfied and that they have no additional rights to the property. If you are self-financing the basement remodel, make sure you get the lien released when you pay a contractor or supplier. Most contractors, suppliers, and sta-tionery stores have the forms.

If you'd like to know more about mortgages, lenders, liens, and other financial aspects of homes, get my book, *The Complete Idiot's Guide to Building Your Own Home* (Alpha Books, 2002).

Living in a Construction Zone

I've covered how much finishing your base-ment will cost in financial terms. Now let's consider how much it might cost in living terms. Here are three questions, and discus-sions of each, that you should answer before you actually begin the remodeling process. I don't want to encourage projects that break up otherwise happy homes!

Construction is a mess. How long can you live with it?

How Inconvenient?

Face it: Remodeling your home's basement will be inconvenient. Maybe you're doing the work in evenings and on weekends. Or you've hired a contractor to do the work during the week. The side yard will be torn up by a bulldozer clawing for access to your foundation. Or it will be stacked high with lumber, plumbing fixtures, and other expensive things.

On the Level

Remodelers recommend that you document your project in photographs. Not only does it illustrate progress, but it also helps you find problems later. If a leak develops in the ceiling or walls, you can pull out the progress pictures and determine what might be the source—and how best to get to it.

I don't know your exact situation, what you'll be doing in your basement, who'll do the work, or how you'll pay for it, so I can't guess how inconvenient the job might become. But I can make an educated guess! Unless you're hiring an angelic contractor who will finish the job while you're off to the Bahamas, chances are you *will* face inconvenience.

Consider your project from this level: inconvenience. Think of it as not only your personal inconvenience but that of other members of your living group. Then, do what you can to minimize the inconvenience. You may decide to hire someone to help you get the job done faster. Or you may want to take a short vacation while a contractor tears up your driveway. Do whatever you can to minimize the inconvenience of remodeling to you and those with whom you share living space.

How Long?

The famous "Murphy" of "Murphy's Law" fame must have realized his truth while attempting to finish a basement. "Anything that can go wrong will, at the worst possible time." Plan as you might, a moisture problem, the wrong materials, a late inspection, an unexpected cost increase, or some other life event can s-l-o-w progress on finishing your basement.

The best advice is to do the project as quickly as possible, even if you have to do it in stages. Delays become inertia and projects don't seem to get done. Life intercedes and that basement project is moved to the back burner. The solution is to make sure you have not only the money, but the available time to complete your basement.

Construction Zone

Living in a construction zone can be hazardous to your health—and to the health of kids, pets, and other critters. Make sure that the last job of each day—yours or your contractor's—is to make sure that the site is safe. Otherwise, lock the door to the basement.

The day will come when decorative stairs bring you and guests to your new finished basement. Keep the faith!

What If?

Stuff happens. What if you just can't finish your basement remodeling? The money runs out. Illness stops the labor force. A new job opportunity requires that you be elsewhere—next Tuesday! What can you do?

The answer is: the best you can. If you've broken your project into sub-projects you'll always be near a finishing point. If not, consider hiring (or begging) someone to continue the work for you. If all else fails, just stop where you are. You're finishing your basement to increase enjoyment for you and your living group. If the task becomes counterproductive, take some time to rethink the project and how it fits in your life. Maybe you just need a short vacation from it.

Gosh, I hope you don't think I'm trying to talk you out of finishing your basement. I'm really not! I want you to consider both the plusses and the minuses of it *before* you actually

start buying things and installing them. Make sure you've planned thoroughly, estimated costs accurately, figured out exactly how you're going to pay for it, and considered potential problems. Doing so will increase your chances of success as well as your enjoyment of your new living space. And that's what it's all about.

The Least You Need to Know

- ◆ Answering four simple questions about your basement remodel can cut costs and increase your enjoyment.

- ◆ Use a materials list to estimate specific costs of finishing your basement.

- ◆ Make sure you know where the money's coming from before you begin to spend it on remodeling.

- ◆ Consider potential problems and find solutions before they are needed.

In This Chapter

◆ Understanding the building and remodeling process

◆ Making sure you get your permits and follow building codes

◆ Getting the basement ready for finishing

◆ Sealing the basement against moisture

Permits and Preparation

It would be great if you didn't need to follow building codes and buy a building permit when constructing or remodeling a home. Think of all the time and money you'd save. However, would you buy or live in a home that wasn't built under building safety codes? What if the prior owner tried to save money on wiring by using inferior materials?

This chapter covers how and when you'll need a building permit for finishing your basement as well as how to follow local codes. In addition, it begins the remodeling process by showing you how to prepare for finishing your basement. You'll be getting ready for new construction and taking care of any final problems.

The Remodeling Process

Of course, you're not the first homeowner to finish a basement. That's good. That means there's a proven process for remodeling that you can follow to reduce time and costs. Whether you're working with a general contractor, hiring subcontractors, or doing all the work yourself, you can put the remodeling process or sequence to work for you.

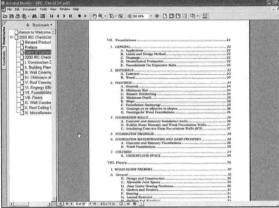

The International Residential Code (IRC) checklist published by the International Code Council.

Remodeling Sequence

Here's the typical remodeling sequence for larger jobs such as finishing a basement:

1. Structural changes (walls, subfloors, doors, windows)

Wall framing over an exposed wall pipe.

2. Rough utility changes (wiring, plumbing, HVAC, cable)

Framing around an exposed ceiling pipe.

Exposed heating duct.

Framing an exposed heating duct.

3. Insulation
4. Ceiling and wall covering
5. Painting
6. Electrical fixtures and lighting
7. Cabinets, shelves, and countertops
8. Flooring
9. Major appliances
10. Furniture
11. Decor

Decorative touches will personalize your finished basement.

Chapters 6 through 14 will take you step by step through this process on a relatively direct path. Except for Chapter 8, which guides you through roughing in electrical (job #2 on our list), then jumps to installing electrical fixtures and lighting (job #6), the coming chapters are sequential and highly illustrated to make the tasks easier. The following charts are offered to help acquaint you with the lumber and fasteners you will be using to finish your basement.

Nominal size (in.)	American standard (in.)
1 × 3	$25/32 \times 25/8$
1 × 4	$25/32 \times 35/8$
1 × 6	$25/32 \times 55/8$
1 × 8	$25/32 \times 71/2$
1 × 10	$25/32 \times 91/2$
1 × 12	$25/32 \times 111/2$
2 × 4	$15/8 \times 35/8$
2 × 6	$15/8 \times 55/8$
2 × 8	$15/8 \times 71/2$
2 × 10	$15/8 \times 91/2$
2 × 12	$15/8 \times 111/2$
3 × 8	$25/8 \times 71/2$
3 × 10	$25/8 \times 91/2$
3 × 12	$25/8 \times 111/2$
4 × 12	$35/8 \times 111/2$
4 × 16	$35/8 \times 151/2$
6 × 12	$51/2 \times 111/2$
6 × 16	$51/2 \times 151/2$
6 × 18	$51/2 \times 171/2$
8 × 16	$71/2 \times 151/2$
8 × 20	$71/2 \times 191/2$
8 × 24	$71/2 \times 231/2$

Nominal sizing of lumber.

Nominal size (in.)	Actual length in feet								
	8	10	12	14	16	18	20	22	24
1 × 2		1²/3	2	2¹/3	2²/3	3	3¹/2	3²/3	4
1 × 3		2¹/2	3	3¹/2	4	4¹/2	5	5¹/2	6
1 × 4	2³/4	3¹/3	4	4²/3	5¹/3	6	6²/3	7¹/3	8
1 × 5		4¹/6	5	5⁵/6	6²/3	7¹/2	8¹/3	9¹/6	10
1 × 6	4	5	6	7	8	9	10	11	12
1 × 7		5⁵/8	7	8¹/6	9¹/3	10¹/2	11²/3	12⁵/6	14
1 × 8	5¹/3	6²/3	8	9¹/3	10²/3	12	13¹/3	14²/3	16
1 × 10	6²/3	8¹/3	10	11²/3	13¹/3	15	16²/3	18¹/3	20
1 × 12	8	10	12	14	16	18	20	22	24
1¹/4 × 4		4¹/6	5	5⁵/6	6²/3	7¹/2	8¹/3		10
1¹/4 × 6		6¹/4	7¹/2	8³/4	10	11¹/4	12¹/2	13³/4	15
1¹/4 × 8		8¹/3	10	11²/3	13¹/3	15	16²/3	18¹/3	20
1¹/4 × 10		10⁵/12	12¹/2	14⁷/12	16²/3	18³/4	20⁵/6	22¹¹/12	25
1¹/4 × 12		12¹/2	15	17¹/2	20	22¹/2	25	27¹/2	30
1¹/2 × 4	4	5	6	7	8	9	10	11	12
1¹/2 × 6	6	7¹/2	9	10¹/2	12	13¹/2	15	16¹/2	18
1¹/2 × 8	8	10	12	14	16	18	20	22	24
1¹/2 × 10	10	12¹/2	15	17¹/2	20	22¹/2	25	27¹/2	30
1¹/2 × 12	12	15	18	21	24	27	30	33	36
2 × 4	5¹/3	6²/3	8	9¹/3	10¹/3	12	13¹/3	14²/3	16
2 × 6	8	10	12	14	16	18	20	22	24
2 × 8	10²/3	13¹/3	16	18²/3	21¹/3	24	26²/3	29¹/3	32
2 × 10	13¹/3	16²/3	20	23¹/3	26²/3	30	33¹/3	36²/3	40
2 × 12	16	20	24	28	32	36	40	44	48
3 × 6	12	15	18	21	24	27	30	33	36
3 × 8	16	20	24	28	32	36	40	44	48
3 × 10	20	25	30	35	40	45	50	55	60
3 × 12	24	30	36	42	48	54	60	66	72
4 × 4	10²/3	13¹/3	16	18²/3	21¹/3	24	26²/3	29¹/3	32
4 × 6	16	20	24	28	32	36	40	44	48
4 × 8	21¹/3	26²/3	32	37¹/3	42²/3	48	53¹/3	58²/3	64
4 × 10	26²/3	33¹/3	40	46²/3	53¹/3	60	66²/3	73¹/3	80
4 × 12	32	40	48	56	64	72	80	88	96

Calculating board feet.

Common Wire Nails

Size	Length	Gauge	Approx. No. to Lb.	Size	Length	Gauge	Approx. No. to Lb.
2D	1 In.	No. 15	876	10D	3 In.	No. 9	69
3D	1¼	14	568	12D	3¼	9	63
4D	1½	12½	316	16D	3½	8	49
5D	1¾	12½	271	20D	4	6	31
6D	2	11½	181	30D	4½	5	24
7D	2¼	11½	161	40D	5	4	18
8D	2½	10¼	106	50D	5½	3	14
9D	2¾	10¼	96	60D	6	2	11

Flooring Brads

Size	Length	Gauge	Approx. No. to Lb.
6D	2 In.	No. 11	157
7D	2¼	11	139
8D	2½	10	99
9D	2¾	10	90
10D	3	9	69
12D	3¼	8	54
16D	3½	7	43
20D	4	6	31

Finishing Nails

Size	Length	Gauge	Approx. No. to Lb.
2D	1 In.	No. 16½	1351
3D	1¼	15½	807
4D	1½	15	584
5D	1¾	15	500
6D	2	13	309
7D	2¼	13	238
8D	2½	12½	189
9D	2¾	12½	172
10D	3	11½	121
12D	3¼	11½	113
16D	3½	11	90
20D	4	10	62

Smooth & Barbed Box Nails

Size	Length	Gauge	Approx. No. to Lb.
2D	1 In.	No. 15½	1010
3D	1¼	14½	635
4D	1½	14	473
5D	1¾	14	406
6D	2	12½	236
7D	2¼	12½	210
8D	2½	11½	145
9D	2¾	11½	132
10D	3	10½	94
12D	3¼	10½	88
16D	3½	10	71
20D	4	9	52
30D	4½	9	46
40D	5	8	35

Casing Nails

Size	Length	Gauge	Approx. No. to Lb.
2D	1 In.	No. 15½	1010
3D	1¼	14½	635
4D	1½	14	473
5D	1¾	14	406
6D	2	12½	236
7D	2¼	12½	210
8D	2½	11½	145
9D	2¾	11½	132
10D	3	10½	94
12D	3¼	10½	87
16D	3½	10	71
20D	4	9	52
30D	4½	9	46

Nail types and sizes.

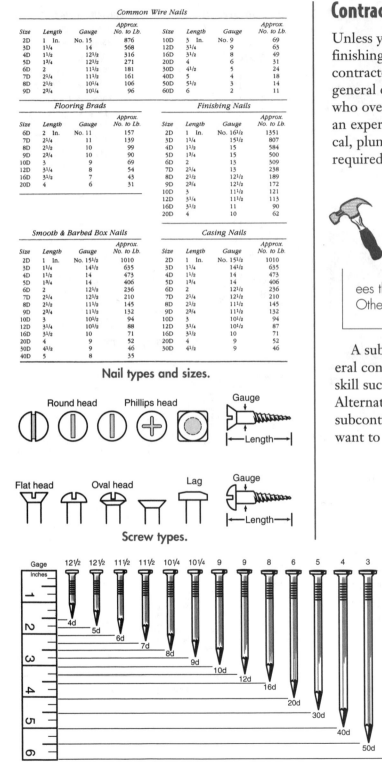

Screw types.

Nail lengths.

Contractors and Subs

Unless you plan to do all the work yourself, finishing a basement requires contractors, sub-contractors, or hired labor. A contractor or general contractor is a construction manager who oversees your entire project, and often is an experienced tradesperson (carpentry, electrical, plumbing) as well. A licensed contractor is required to have business experience as well.

Construction Zone

Make sure that the contractor or subcontractor you hire has adequate worker's compensation insurance for any employees that work on your remodeling job. Otherwise, *you* may be liable for injuries.

A subcontractor typically works for a general contractor by providing a specific trade or skill such as electrical or plumbing service. Alternatively, you, the homeowner, can hire a subcontractor directly to tackle jobs you don't want to or feel qualified to do yourself.

If you have the needed skills but need some help, you can hire labor. It may be a handyperson, a college student, or even a relative or friend to help you with the physical labor of remodeling.

In any case, part of preparing for finishing your basement is making sure you have or can hire the skills and labor needed to do the job quickly, efficiently, and on budget.

Suppliers

For smaller remodeling jobs, spending a weekend morning buying materials is sufficient. However, remodeling a basement into living space typically requires more materials—and that means you should shop around for the best prices and delivery options. You may be fortunate and find a single supplier nearby that can furnish you with all lumber, utility, and finishing materials needed at reasonable prices. In most cases, however, it will take two or three suppliers to get everything you need.

 **On the Level**

How can you find the best suppliers for your remodeling job? Visit them for smaller jobs. You will soon learn by experience which suppliers treat customers well, are helpful, and offer practical advice. Go in asking about a plumbing or wiring job and you'll come out with a low-cost education.

Signing Contracts

Depending on the size of your basement remodeling project, you may need to sign contracts with lenders, contractors, subcontractors, and suppliers. Should you? Yes.

However, make sure you read over and understand the terms of the contract. You may have total trust in a specific person you're dealing with, but contracts typically are written in favor of the contractor. It just makes good sense to read contracts over and understand them before signing. And make sure that you get all designs, specifications, requirements, and other facts in writing. Verbal contracts are rarely enforceable.

Codes and Permits

Like it or not, most larger remodeling projects require that you follow local building codes and pay for a building permit. Actually, it's for your own good. Codes are standards, and permits are a way of tracking remodeling done to a specific structure. An inspection is the physical review of a project by someone with knowledge of building codes and regulations.

Building Plans

It all starts with a building *plan*, a detailed drawing of exactly what you (or your contractors) will be doing to change an existing structure. It will include a drawing of the structure as it is today as well as the planned changes. Depending on how extensive the remodeling is, building plans will include some or all of the following:

- ◆ Framing plan
- ◆ Floor plans
- ◆ Wiring plan
- ◆ Plumbing plan
- ◆ Interior elevations
- ◆ Section drawings (show part of a building as it would appear if cut through by a vertical plane)
- ◆ Specifications list
- ◆ Materials list

Chief Architect and other residential design software programs can develop a materials list for remodeling projects.

Materials lists can be exported to a spreadsheet.

A trip to your local building department will tell you what permits will be needed, what plans you'll need to supply, and what building codes you must follow to finish your basement.

Building Codes

The purpose of building codes is to ensure that a structure meets standardized health and safety requirements set up to protect you, your neighbors, and anyone who buys the house in the future. Contractors are required to know and build or remodel following these codes. If you're doing some or all of your own remodeling you, too, must follow the codes.

Fortunately, local building codes are available through local building departments. Most are standardized throughout the nation with local variations based on local needs (for earthquake construction, tornado construction, etc.).

Building Permits

A building permit is an official document provided by a local building jurisdiction that permits you to build or remodel *if* you do so following approved plans and local building codes.

Do You Need a Building Permit?

Local building codes in various locations don't always agree on what requires a building permit and what doesn't. However, here are some typical home remodeling jobs that *don't* require a permit:

◆ Storage and tool sheds

◆ Fences under 6 feet in height

◆ Painting, papering, and finish work

◆ Window awnings and shade structures

◆ Prefab swimming pools

As you can see, most remodeling work done to finish a basement (except painting) probably *will* require a building permit. Check with your city or county building department for specific requirements before starting the job.

Most jurisdictions require copies of your building plans and assurances that you will follow local building codes during the project. To enforce compliance, building departments will require that the project be inspected by an employee of the department, called a building inspector, and approved or signed off at specific stages of the project. If you continue construction without the needed sign off, the inspector will probably require that you remove materials so the prior work can be inspected. Ouch! In the long run it's best to find out what permits are required and what codes need to be followed, and to allow inspections as required.

If you've hired a general or remodeling contractor to do most or all of the work, he or she will take care of the building permits for you and ensure that codes are followed. That's what contractors get paid to do.

Preparing for Construction

Congratulations! You've been issued the appropriate building permits and know what codes you need to follow. You can now begin preparing for remodeling your basement.

What's the first step? Getting the unfinished basement ready for construction. That means removing any existing components as needed, exterminating any insects or other critters, and checking for carbon monoxide, radon, asbestos, and other health hazards.

Removing Existing Components

In many parts of the United States and Canada, the unfinished basement serves as the site for the bulky heating furnace and air conditioning systems. Depending on your remodeling plans, these components may need to be moved either within the basement or to another floor in the home. This is a job for HVAC experts, but you can assist or at least direct them in the project. For many basement remodels it's a matter of enclosing the equipment where it is. For other homes, some of the equipment or ducting will be relocated. Just make sure you don't close off access in case the system needs service or replacement in the future.

If your basement has walls that you won't be using, they will need to be removed before remodeling begins. Make sure the walls are not load bearing, supporting the floor above. If you need to move a supporting post, consider hiring a contractor to do the work for you as there may be issues that can jeopardize your home's structural integrity.

Insects and Other Pests

Unfinished basements often become a breeding ground for various insects and even rodents. Because they're uninvited house guests, you have the right to evict them at will. Now is a good time. In some cases, cleaning the basement and spraying it with approved insecticides will take care of the problem. In extreme cases, hire a licensed exterminator to prepare your unfinished basement for remodeling.

Carbon Monoxide

Carbon monoxide is a by-product of burning. That means carbon monoxide is present around fireplaces, furnaces, gas appliances, and other combustion appliances as well as in garages where a car's engine is running. High amounts of carbon monoxide can be a health hazard to humans and pets. Alarms are available at larger hardware stores to test for the presence of excessive levels of carbon monoxide.

Radon

Radon is an odorless gas released when traces of uranium in the ground decay. Outside the home, radon quickly dissipates in the atmosphere. Underneath a home, radon gas can build up and become a health hazard, especially to those who smoke cigarettes or have respiratory problems.

Fortunately, you can buy a radon test or alarm kit at larger building materials outlets and use it to find out if hazardous amounts of radon gas (4 picocuries per liter of air) are present. Instructions with the testers and alarms will tell you what to do next.

Asbestos

Asbestos, unfortunately, isn't as easy to detect. Asbestos was used in many building materials until about 20 years ago when the health hazards were identified. It was used in insulation, flooring, and other materials. Only airborne asbestos poses a health risk. That means removing some building materials in older homes can release asbestos particles into the atmosphere and potentially cause health problems.

Construction prior to about 1985 may have asbestos in building products such as ceiling insulation.

Contractors trained and licensed for asbestos removal may be the best option if you suspect that your unfinished basement has asbestos. Check your local telephone book under "Asbestos Abatement & Removal Service" or "Asbestos Consulting & Testing" to learn how to have your home inspected for this hazard.

Sealing Your Basement

Finally, make sure that your basement is sealed from moisture. I discussed the requirements and tests in Chapter 2. Now it's time to do whatever work is necessary to ensure that your basement is and remains dry. Here are some suggestions:

♦ Test for water seepage through the walls and floor as described in Chapter 2.

♦ Make sure the foundation's exterior has sufficient drainage to keep water out of the basement.

♦ If necessary, install drain lines around the exterior footing or under the concrete floor slab to ensure that surfaces stay dry.

♦ As needed, install, move, or repair any sump pumps to keep moisture out of the basement.

♦ Make any masonry or other repairs needed to the basement walls and floor in preparation for finishing.

♦ Seal the basement walls and floor with waterproofing materials as needed to keep the basement dry.

On the Level

Remodelers recommend carefully inspecting all foundation walls prior to starting the job, especially for stress crack leaks, rod hole leaks, and other obvious damage. Many remodelers use epoxy injection for filling and sealing cracks and holes. Ask your building material supplier about this process.

That's about it. You've planned your new basement and prepared it for remodeling including finding resources to make the job easier. You have the needed permits and know what building codes apply. You've figured how much it will cost and how you're going to pay for it. The next step is to start remodeling!

The Least You Need to Know

♦ Remodeling is a proven process with specific steps that are successfully completed by do-it-yourselfers every day.

♦ Make sure you visit the local building department soon to find out what permits are needed and which codes must be followed.

♦ Building plans are your map; comprehensive plans make the trip easier and more trouble free.

♦ Before starting a basement remodel, make sure you remove any existing pests or hazardous materials.

In This Part

Part 2

Remodeling Your Basement

Okay, it's time to quit doodling and start nailing something! This part shows you how to turn that empty space into a living space. It includes structural remodeling, plumbing, wiring, lighting, plus finishing walls, ceilings, and floors. Along the way you'll get loads of tips from professional basement remodelers—tips you can use to make your basement even better.

Don't worry that you've never pounded a nail or wired a light. It's okay. I'll show you how to do it all. You'll lcarn what to ask for when you buy materials and how to install them. Grab a hammer and let's head for the basement!

In This Chapter

- ◆ Preparing for a new floor
- ◆ Installing stairways
- ◆ Building walls
- ◆ Putting in doors and windows

Chapter 6

Structural Remodeling

It's time to grab a hammer and start pounding on something! That's the fun part of finishing your basement. Of course, you'll probably want to first determine what needs pounding.

In this chapter, you'll learn how to pound away to install a new subfloor, stairs, walls, doors, windows, and other structural components of your basement. Fortunately, the plans you made in Chapter 3 will show you *where* everything goes. And this chapter will show you *how*. So strap on your tool belt (optional) and let's go find something to pound!

Preparing the Subfloor

That nice carpet, wood, or tile floor you walk on isn't actually the floor. It's the top component of your home's flooring system. Supporting the flooring material—and your every step—is the *subfloor*. Below that are the floor joists (for wood floor systems) or a concrete slab (for concrete systems). Together, they make up your home's floor.

Chances are, your unfinished basement doesn't have flooring materials such as carpet, wood, or tile. Instead, the wood or concrete subfloor may be exposed. That means you'll have to get this surface ready for flooring materials. You won't install the flooring materials until Chapter 11, but you need to make sure the subfloor is ready now because it will be more difficult to fix any problems after you've installed new walls, stairs, and other components that sit atop the subfloor.

> **Deeper Meaning** _____
>
> **Subfloor** is typically made of plywood or oriented strand boards attached to the joists. The finish floor is laid over the subfloor. The subfloor also can be made of concrete.

Concrete

Many basements are constructed of concrete to withstand the exterior wall pressures caused by being below ground level. In addition, concrete can withstand moisture better than wood. So the majority of basement walls are made of either poured concrete or masonry blocks. Concrete basements typically have a poured concrete flooring system in what's called a slab.

Concrete block is a popular building material for foundations and basement walls.

Any movement of ground below or near the concrete slab floor can cause the massive slab to crack. That's why thick concrete such as that used in basement walls and floors is reinforced with metal bars called rebar. Exactly how much rebar is used and in what pattern depends on local building codes and the size of the slab. Some building codes allow a wire reinforcement mesh to be installed instead.

Because concrete is porous, moisture can come up through the floor (or through walls), ruining any flooring material you've installed. So preparing the subfloor for flooring materials means sealing it against moisture. It also means making sure the surface is level so that the flooring will be level.

So you can see the job ahead if your unfinished basement has a concrete slab floor: Seal and level it. In Chapter 2, I described a simple way of testing whether your concrete basement has moisture and finding its source. Fortunately, there are many quality waterproofing sealers available on the market. Some are brushed on or spread with rollers. Others are vapor barrier sheets that are installed on top of the subfloor. Once installed, take the moisture test again to make sure that no moisture will damage flooring material.

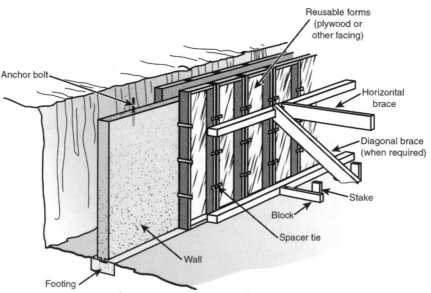

Here's how concrete walls are framed and poured.

Construction Zone _____

Make sure that you use concrete patch to fix any cracks in the basement floor before installing the waterproofing sealer and/or vapor barrier.

How do you level a concrete slab subfloor? Hopefully, the unfinished floor in your basement is relatively level. If not, you can either build a new wood subfloor over it, leveling as needed or you can apply a floor leveler.

Here are the steps to installing a new wood subfloor:

1. Stretch a plastic moisture barrier over the repaired concrete, overlapping as needed to form a strong seal. (Make sure you install vapor barrier material correctly. The protective side—often silver or black in color—should be on the side farthest from you when you install it. Otherwise you may trap moisture against drywall, flooring, or under a subfloor.)

2. Install 2-by-4-inch wood members called sleepers as a horizontal frame over the subfloor.

3. Install ¼-inch plywood over the sleepers as the new subfloor.

4. Install the new flooring materials on the new subfloor per instructions in Chapter 11.

There are a couple of reasons for considering a new wood subfloor over a concrete subfloor. First, some flooring materials such as solid hardwood are difficult to attach to concrete. A wood subfloor is a better base. Second, the new subfloor can be installed to bring the entire subfloor to the same level. Keep in mind, however, that installing the second subfloor cuts the available height of your basement room by about 2½ inches.

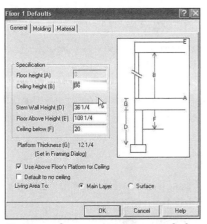

Design software programs can help design basement walls.

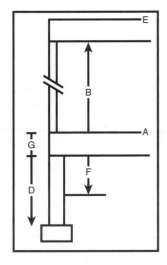

Defining basement wall components.

On the Level _____

If you plan to run lots of cables or new plumbing and can't do so overhead or in walls easily, a new wood subfloor offers space between the sleepers for pipe and wiring to be run.

Applying a floor leveler is much easier. It's a product that you mix with water, pour on concrete, and spread as level as possible. It begins to harden within about 15 minutes and can be used to build the surface up as much as 1 inch. You can use it for a specific area or an entire floor. Follow the manufacturer's recommendations.

Wood

A wood basement subfloor typically is easier to prepare for flooring. The goals are the same: seal and level it. Sealing is done with a moisture barrier such as plastic sheeting or builder's felt depending on whether moisture is a problem. The subfloor can be leveled by installing a thin plywood over the top of the floor.

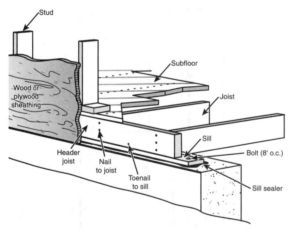

Cross-section of a typical wood-framed floor.

Plywood and particleboard are popular wood subfloor components.

On the Level _____

If the wood floor squeaks, install ring-shank nails through the subfloor and into flooring joists. You can identify the location of the joists by looking for rows of nail heads.

If your wood floor requires additional insulation, refer to Chapter 10 for information on various insulating materials and how to install them.

Remodeling Stairways

Chances are that your basement already has a stairway leading down to it. However, you may not feel that it is adequate for the additional traffic it will get as you finish your basement. So let's take a look at how to install or remodel stairways.

The three primary types of stairways are straight, landing, and circular. A straight stairway is made of three or more sets of treads (horizontal steps) and risers (vertical tread supports). A landing stairway has at least one area with a deeper tread, called a landing. A landing typically is used to break up a long stairway into shorter ones for safety or to allow a turn in the stairway. A circular stairway is a space saver, requiring less space for installation. However, circular stairways make moving furniture between floors difficult.

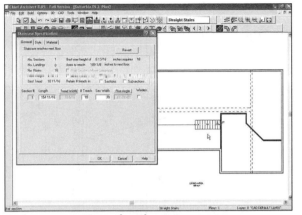

First select the stair type.

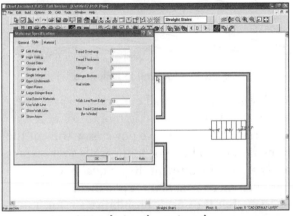

Next design the stair style.

There are numerous regulations and guidelines for stairways. For example, there must be at least 6 feet 8 inches of headroom, treads must be at least 10 inches deep, risers must be 7¼ to 7¾ inches high, landings must be at least 36 inches wide. There's lots more depending on local code, the living space the stairway will serve, and the run or horizontal length of the stairway.

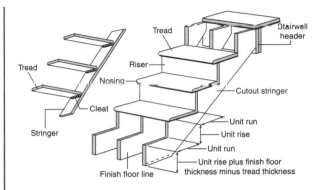

Typical components of stairs.

Fortunately, the plans you had drawn or drew up yourself according to local code (see Chapter 3) spelled out the requirements for your new stairway. Maybe you're adding to or remodeling an existing stairway, or maybe you're ripping it all out and starting over. In any case, the plans tell you what needs to be done. To simplify, here are the typical steps for installing stairways:

1. Frame the top landing and support posts *or* cut and frame an opening in the main floor.

2. Cut and install the diagonal stair carriages.

3. Reinforce the carriages with supports.

4. Install all landings, treads, and risers.

5. Install handrails and balusters included in the plans.

6. Trim and finish.

Of course, there are numerous variations to this procedure. However, installing stairs typically follows these steps.

Alternatively, you may be adding an exterior stairway to the basement through a cellar door. This job requires more work as you cut a large hole in the foundation wall, pour or build steps, and install the cellar door on its own foundation. Because you are changing the foundation wall, you probably will need a structural engineer and possibly a contractor to help you get the required building permit and do the job.

Cellar stairways are built in a similar process to other stairways. Cellar doors can be purchased from larger building material suppliers and installed on their own block or concrete foundation following the manufacturer's instructions.

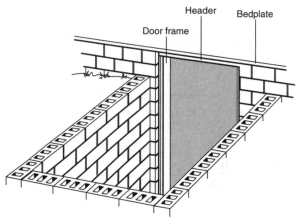

Typical exterior stair entry.

Installing New Walls

Your finished basement plans probably call for installing new walls. A wall is a vertical structure member which encloses, divides, supports, or protects a building or room. Your basement's exterior walls are the foundation walls. You'll be installing interior walls.

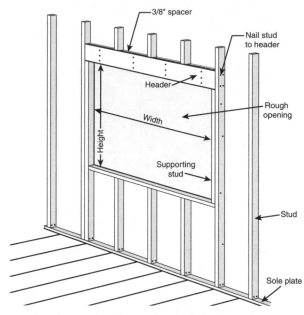

Framing an interior wall to include a window.

Tools needed for wall construction are basic: a saw to cut and a fastening tool to connect materials. An inexpensive power saw will cut the time needed to build or frame walls so it's typically a good investment. Buy a quality carpenter's hammer for nailing. A pneumatic nail gun is faster, but the cost is prohibitive for most do-it-yourselfers. You can rent one by the hour, day, or week from larger rental centers, or borrow one from your flooring supplier, if available.

As homes are built, wall framing is fastened to the wooden subfloor below. However, when installing walls over concrete, special nails or tools are needed to fasten the wood to the concrete floor. Use masonry nails or masonry screws (in pre-drilled holes) to fasten wood to concrete. Alternatively, there are adhesive products that can be spread below the wall during erection to bond the wall and floor.

New wall framing also must be attached to foundation walls. As with floors, you can fasten the wood wall frame to the concrete wall using masonry nails or screws. However, remember to prepare the foundation wall surface first with moisture barrier.

Framing lumber is sold at building
material and lumber stores.

There are two common methods of building
new walls in a basement. One is to fasten the
bottom horizontal piece (the bottom plate) to the
floor, the top plate to the joists directly above,
then cut and install vertical studs between them,
following the plans. The other method is to
simultaneously mark the bottom and top plates
for the location of all studs, then fasten the studs
between the plates as they all lay horizontally on
the floor, finally lifting the top plate into place.
Insert wood shims between the top plate and
joists, make sure the wall is straight, then nail
both the top and bottom plates in place.

The second method, raising the wall, typically is easier. However, the first one, building
the wall in place, makes more sense if the wall
height may need to be varied due to an uneven
ceiling or floor.

Metal Studs

Metal studs are increasing in popularity, especially in basement remodels. They are straight,
cheaper than wood, faster to install, and are
perfect for non-load-bearing walls. However,
you still need wood studs wherever you will be
nailing prehung doors or cabinets into a stud,
or need to hang things on walls by attaching
them to a stud. Metal-stud walls require wall
anchors for hanging heavy objects.

Remember, that these are *non*-load-bearing
walls. That is, they aren't designed to support
part of the house above. That's what posts and
pillars in the basement are for. Don't attempt
to move a load-bearing post or wall without
professional help. Instead, plan around them,
incorporating the posts into walls if possible.

Posts are required to support the floors above.

Wall framing consists of vertical studs installed
between the top and bottom horizontal plates.

False walls can hide pipes and equipment.

Wood framing also protects the interior from moisture.

This soffit hides overhead pipe.

A second view of the soffit framing.

Installing Doors and Windows

Your new basement will need doors and doorways for moving between rooms as well as windows to allow in available light. In addition, windows may be required as emergency exits in basement bedrooms where there are no other exits. Your basement plans will specify what doors and windows go where, or you may be installing them as you go. In either case, let's take a closer look at how doors and windows are installed in basements.

Open Doorways and Archways

The easiest door to install is the one that isn't there. That is, a doorway can be left open for people to pass between rooms more easily. Many basement designs have rooms with doorways instead of doors, depending on the functions of each room. Obviously, the bathroom should have a door on it for privacy. However, a basement finished into a small apartment may not need a door in to a bedroom or kitchen.

An archway is a fancy doorway with a curved structural member, called an arch, above the opening. Archways are especially practical in basements where headroom is at a premium because archways don't require a rectangular header or support above them.

Because a doorway or archway doesn't have a door on hinges, framing them is relatively easy. Archways present some challenge as they require a curve, a difficult form to get from dimensional wood. However by using a thin piece of plywood as the curved base, you can cut a top plate and cripples (short studs) to conform to the doorway.

Prehung Doors and Windows

Doors and windows are commodities. That is, you can go down to your favorite building material store and buy doors in their own frame all ready for insertion in a doorway. Windows, too, come prehung.

Selecting a prehung door.

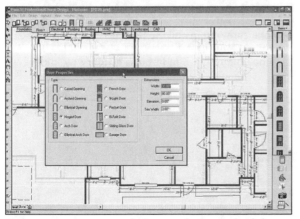

Software programs can help you place standard doors.

Doors come in standard widths of 30, 32, and 36 inches. Here's how to install prehung doors:

1. Set the door unit in the framed opening and insert wood shims near the hinges until the frame is plumb.

2. Nail through the door unit frame and wood shim into the doorway frame.

3. Install shims around the perimeter of the door unit frame making sure that the door operates smoothly and is level and plumb.

4. Remove the excess shims.

House Framing Tips

Wood stud framing is very popular, especially with remodels to existing basements. Components are standardized and construction is quick and relatively inexpensive compared to other construction methods. Here are some tips from a professional builder on working with wood stud framing systems.

Walls for this bathroom are quickly framed using 2 × 4 studs. The room's corner is reinforced with short studs.

Walls typically are built horizontally on the subfloor then raised into position. Wall framing consists of the sole (bottom horizontal) plate, vertical studs, and the horizontal top plate. Openings are left for future doorways.

Make sure you install the one-piece bathtub in the house before framing because you probably won't be able to get it in through a doorway later.

The studs are drilled for wiring and electrical boxes installed on studs.

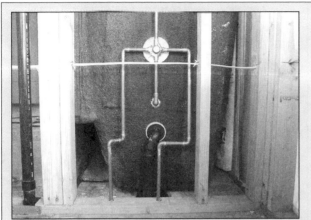

The sole plate is cut so pipes can be run from underneath the house. Cement-slab basements require that pipes run through ceiling and walls. (This is the side of the bathtub seen in the previous figure.)

Plumbing runs through wall framing. This area will become a kitchen with sink, drain, and an electrical connection for the garbage disposal. Notice the metal stud and sole plate covers installed to protect the pipes from future damage.

Solid wood components called headers are installed above doorways and windows to help hold the weight of higher floors. Alternately, short studs called "cripples" can be installed.

The metal box on the left is the return vent that draws air from the home back to the furnace. Warm air will blow through registers in the wall or floor, depending on the subfloor type.

You will be applying finish molding around the opening to cover the frame and shims in Chapter 10.

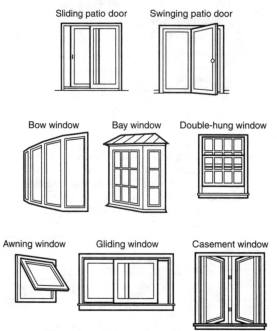

Sliding patio door   Swinging patio door

Bow window   Bay window   Double-hung window

Awning window   Gliding window   Casement window

There is a wide variety of window styles and designs available.

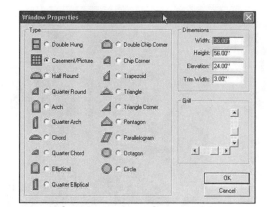

Software programs for remodelers can select standard windows.

Typical prehung windows.

Prehung windows are installed in a similar manner. The primary difference is that the lower edge of the window is shimmed and nailed first, then the sides and top. The manufacturer's installation instructions come with prehung windows and doors to tell you how to install the units.

A beautiful window selection brings sunlight into the partial basement.

The Least You Need to Know

◆ Make sure your basement's subfloor is dry and level before installing flooring materials.

◆ Stairways are more difficult to build or remodel than other basement components, but do-it-yourselfers who follow the building plans can install them.

◆ Framing basement walls can be built in place or built and raised depending on which fits your basement.

◆ Prehung door and window units make installation easier than buying and installing components.

In This Chapter

◆ Getting ready to plumb your basement

◆ Installing water and drain lines

◆ Placing plumbing fixtures

◆ Putting in heating and air conditioning systems

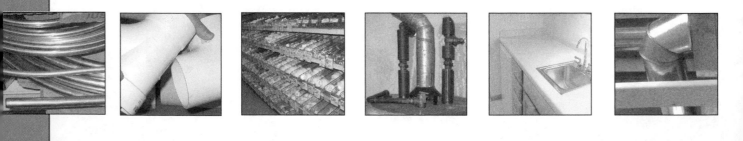

Plumbing Your Basement

To make your basement livable you'll want plumbing. A bathroom needs hot and cold running water, a toilet, and maybe a bath tub or shower. A kitchen requires running water for washing dishes and preparing food. Plumbing is the system of pipes and fixtures that handle the water in your home.

Your house already has a plumbing system, so it may be easy to tie the new system into the old. But how? With what? And what about comfort systems like heating and air conditioning? These are the topics of this chapter. In it you'll learn how to plan and install plumbing and comfort systems in your new basement.

Planning the Plumbing

Plumbing brings in fresh water and removes waste water. The fresh water system is called the supply system. It brings water from the main source (city water or private well) and distributes it to sinks, toilets, tubs, and other plumbing fixtures.

Actually, the supply system includes two sets of pipes, one for cold water and one for hot water. The hot water system heats up a portion of the supply water in one or more tanks inside your home. It then distributes it to sinks, tubs, and showers that require both hot and cold water.

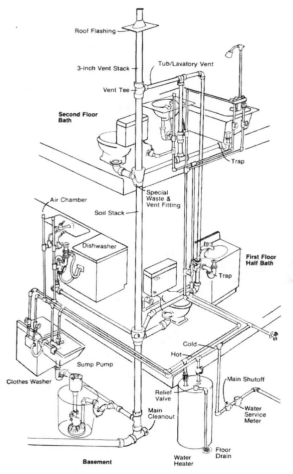

Typical residential plumbing system.

Where does it all go? Waste water from sinks, toilets, and other fixtures are removed from your home by the drain-waste system. Because gases can build up in waste, this system also includes a venting system. Together, the waste system is called a drain-waste-vent or *DWV* system. You'll see it in action in this chapter.

Deeper Meaning

DWV, an acronym for drain-waste-vent, refers to all or part of the plumbing system that carries waste water from fixtures to the sewer and gases to the roof.

Extending Pipe

If you already have detailed plans drawn up for finishing your home, the plumbing plans will show where new supply and DWV lines go. The plans will probably also show how the new plumbing ties in to the existing system.

Alternatively, you'll need to find where the supply system enters and the DWV line exits the house. The main turnoff valve for the supply system typically is either inside the basement at the wall nearest the street (or well) or just outside the foundation at that point. Many plumbers install a red valve so it easily can be seen in case of an emergency. DWV systems don't have shutoffs. However, their size (2 to 4 inches in diameter) and color (typically black) give their location away.

Pumping When the Lights Go Out

Sump pumps are a practical addition if you're concerned that water may seep through walls and floors, damaging your new basement. However, what if your home has an extended power outage and the pump has no power? Remodeling contractors recommend a water-pressure back-up sump pump for such installations. It works off the water line pressure instead of electricity (which may go out in a storm) or batteries (which can age and die). Ask your plumbing supplier about these units and whether your basement requires one.

Running Uphill

The trick to making a DWV system work correctly is installing pipes at a moderate slope (usually about ¼ inch per running foot) so water and solid waste move together. But how can you do that when the toilet or sink drain is in the basement and below the level of the DWV outlet from the home?

The solution is gravity-flush toilets that use air pressure to push waste up to the DWV line. These are special toilets that cost more to buy and install than standard fixtures. However, they may be the only solution for low bathrooms. Shower drains, too, may require pressurized lines to remove used water. Separate sewage ejection systems can be purchased and installed in your basement bathroom to solve the problem.

In some houses, you may be able to plan the bathroom to be in a location where little or no pressurization is needed for DWV lines. Alternatively, your home may originally have been built with a lower incoming DWV line in anticipation of someone finishing the basement and including a bathroom. Another option is to consider an ecologically friendly toilet that either burns or composts waste so it doesn't need to be connected to the sewer line.

Because DWV lines typically are installed below floors and because basement floors often are of concrete, your basement plans may require digging up and installing the needed sewer lines. To avoid this messy and costly job, consider placing the bathroom and any other rooms that need under-floor plumbing as close as possible to the main DWV line and running needed pipes in false walls and floors.

Selecting Piping

Piping comes in various sizes and materials. Which ones should you use when plumbing your basement? Actually, the answer may be dictated by local building code. Older homes used galvanized steel water pipes and iron DWV lines. However, most modern homes are built using rigid or flexible plastic pipes and fittings such as *ABS*. Over the years, plastic plumbing pipes have proven themselves to be safe, inexpensive, and relatively easy to install. They are especially popular with do-it-yourselfers.

Deeper Meaning

ABS is an acronym for acrylonitrile-butadine-styrene, a material used for rigid black plastic pipe in DWV systems. Another popular material is **PVC**, which stands for polyvinyl chloride.

There is a wide variety of plastic or PVC plumbing fittings available at larger building supply stores.

Galvanized pipe is still popular, especially in locations with hard freezes.

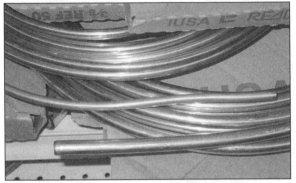

Copper pipe comes in various sizes, requiring special but inexpensive tools and fittings.

Copper pipe is soldered and fittings are installed as connections.

Larger plumbing fittings typically are grouped together in the building material or plumbing store.

Installing Supply Lines

The first step toward installing hot and cold water supply lines in your basement is to decide where the appropriate fixtures will be installed. That is, mark on the floor and the wall framing the location of any sinks, toilets, showers, and other plumbed components. That's where the pipes will deliver their loads.

Next, make sure you know where the water lines will come from. If the flooring system above the basement is open, it may be easy to find and trace lines to a location close to the new installation. For a closed floor, you may need to map and measure the system on the floor above and estimate where the lines will probably be underneath the main floor and above the basement.

If you're working from a full set of remodeling plans you already know this information, indicated in the plumbing plans. They make life easier.

New piping, as mentioned earlier in this chapter, will either be of plastic or copper. Because plastic pipes are larger and easier to work with than copper, most do-it-yourselfers (and most plumbers) prefer plastic. *Which* plastic pipes? If your home is relatively new and uses plastic pipes you can simply use the same size and type to extend the plumbing. The type and grade of pipes will be imprinted on the pipe, though you may have to look on a longer pipe to find readable data. In addition, your remodeling plans may include specifications for the pipe.

Plastic plumbing is easy to assemble. See the following section "Working with Plastic Plumbing."

Assembling copper fittings goes like this:

1. Cut the pipe to length with a pipe cutter.
2. Clean the end of debris with the cutter.
3. Slip the fitting over the pipe.
4. Flare the end of the pipe with the cutter tool.
5. Assemble the components and tighten with a wrench.

Installing Drain Lines

New DWV lines can be joined to the existing system in the same manner. Determine where the lines will run (hopefully, you figured this out already). Drain pipes are cut and assembled using the same process as supply pipes.

Waste drain pipes remove sewage from toilets.

Vent pipes are required by building codes to allow gases trapped in waste lines to vent to outside the home. You may be able to use existing vents that run to the roof if the new components are vented below any existing components. Local building code and your approved plumbing plans will give you more specifics.

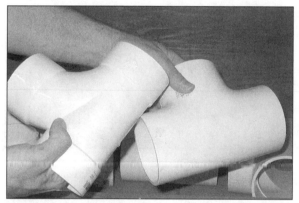

Supply drain pipes carry away gray water from sinks.

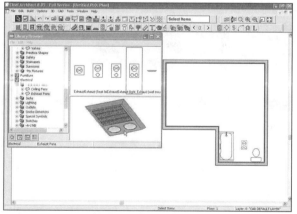

You can use design software to select and plan bathroom ventilation, required by building codes.

Working with Plastic Plumbing

Polyvinyl chloride (PVC) plumbing is not only durable, it is easy to install. You simply cut and glue pieces together. PVC pipe and connectors are very popular in modern housing among professionals and first-timers alike, where local building codes allow. Here's how you can install plastic plumbing.

You can cut PVC pipe with a hand saw, electric saw, or special pipe cutter. Make sure you clamp it firmly in place in a vise to keep it from moving while cutting.

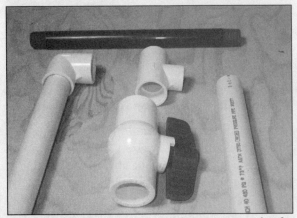

Numerous plumbing pipes and fittings are made of PVC materials in ½-, ¾-, 1-inch, and other sizes used in household plumbing systems.

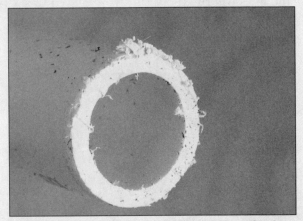

A cut pipe has debris that will keep it from firmly attaching to fittings and fixtures.

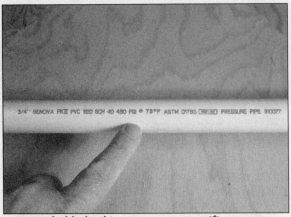

Household plumbing must meet specific pressure and temperature requirements. Make sure the pipe and fittings you purchase meet or exceed the minimum rating or "schedule."

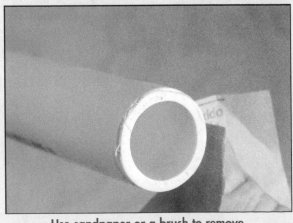

Use sandpaper or a brush to remove debris and smooth the end.

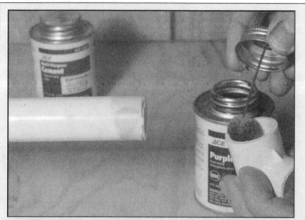

Apply primer to the end of the pipe and the new fitting before installation. The primer cleans any residue and makes the PVC cement adhere better. Follow the primer's label instructions.

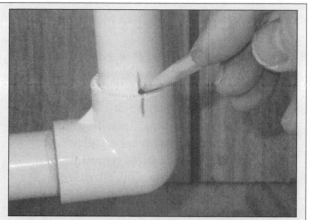

If you need to make sure a pipe is installed in a specific position, first install it without primer or glue and mark the connection on both the fitting and the pipe. Then prime and glue it, matching up the two marks.

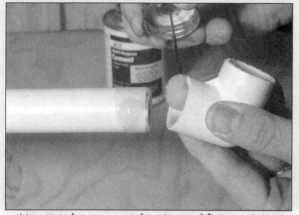

Next, apply cement to the pipe and fitting, wiping away any excess. If you get the glue on your hands, check the can's label for instructions on getting it off.

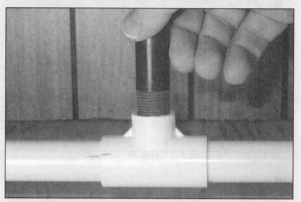

Special fittings are available that allow you to use a screw-in pipe within a cement-fitted PVC system. Remember to first wrap the threaded pipe with plumber's tape for a tight seal.

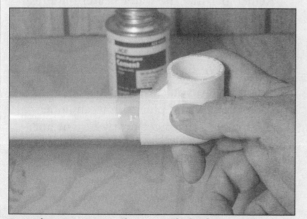

Once the cement is in place, attach the fitting to the pipe. Moving the fitting back and forth helps it slide into position.

You also can install an emergency shutoff at the beginning of the pipe run. Make sure it is accessible (such as under a cabinet, where it easily can be reached and turned).

Installing Fixtures

The plumbing discussed thus far in this chapter is installed in open walls, walls that are framed but don't yet have insulation and drywall on them. This portion of the job is called *roughing in* the plumbing. Installing fixtures (sinks, toilets, showers, tubs) is called *finishing*. Showers and tub enclosures typically are installed before drywall is installed because most don't need drywall behind them; they are attached directly to the wall framing. However, most fixtures are installed later in the process, once the walls are closed. I'll cover installing them all here. Installing kitchen and bathroom cabinets is covered in Chapter 13.

Deeper Meaning

Roughing-in plumbing means installing the basic, hidden parts of a plumbing system while the structure is in the framing stage. **Finish** plumbing is the installation of the visible parts of a plumbing system such as plumbing fixtures and faucets.

Materials and Tools

Fortunately, plumbing fixtures are standardized. That is, most are standard dimensions. The hot and cold water lines to a faucet are a standard distance apart and accept a standard-size pipe from the hot and cold water sources. The opening at the base of a toilet is standard. That means you'll be able to select fixtures based on design and your budget rather than what fits.

Tools for installing plumbing fixtures include wrenches, screwdrivers, and other basic tools. The handiest tools are those specially made to install nuts underneath sink faucets.

Construction Zone

If you're using plastic piping and fittings, make sure you don't overtighten them because they may leak or break.

Installing a Water Heater

Depending on the capacity of your home's existing water heater, you may want to install an additional water heater somewhere in the basement. Under the stairway or in a closet is a good location, though one that is near the new bath and/or kitchen is best.

Connections to and from a typical gas water heater.

Remember that the water heater requires power: gas or electricity. That means you'll also have to install pipes or wiring to power the water heater. Follow the manufacturer's instructions for installation.

Alternatively, you can install a smaller hot tap below a sink and plug it in to an under-counter receptacle to get nearly instant hot water. Single units are much less expensive than water heaters—and easier to install. For small bathrooms, a tankless or on-demand water heater is practical.

Installing Toilets

Standard toilets are relatively easy to install:

1. Install the floor flange, mating it with the toilet DWV pipe.
2. Turn the new toilet over and install the wax gasket.
3. Place the bowl over the flange and nuts.
4. Make sure the bowel is level, then tighten the flange nuts.
5. If necessary, attach the tank to the bowl (some toilets are one piece).
6. Hook up the water supply to the tank.

Installing Sinks

There are three types of sinks: cabinet mounted, wall hung, and freestanding. To install each, first make sure that the pipes are in the correct location and that the flooring, cabinets, and countertops are already installed. Here's how to install a sink:

1. Set the sink in place on the countertop or on the wall hanger, making sure it is level.
2. Install the drain using plumber's putty to seal and tighten from below.
3. Install the faucet with the provided gasket and tighten from below.
4. Install pipes and traps below the sink.
5. Install the water lines to the faucet.
6. Firmly tighten all fittings.

Plumbing makes living in the basement easier.

Installing Other Fixtures

Bathtubs and showers are installed in a similar manner to sinks. All have hot and cold water, a drain system, a base, and walls.

Many shower stalls are single-unit and require special planning prior to installation.

 **On the Level**

Single-unit tubs and showers are so large that you may not be able to get them into rooms once the walls and doors are done. If a single-unit tub won't fit in your basement, make sure you purchase and install separate components.

You can purchase waterproof wall board for lining a shower stall.

Garbage disposals are installed in the same way as a sink drain except that there is a power cord. If a dishwasher is nearby, it will feed debris to the garbage disposal through a drain line.

Installing HVAC

Depending on the design of your existing home, extending its HVAC (heating, ventilation, and air conditioning) system can be relatively easy or quite difficult. It will be difficult if the basement's ceiling is already enclosed.

Tying In to Ducting

If you're certain that the existing HVAC system is powerful enough to handle the comfort needs of the finished basement, you can tie in to the main supply duct or to branches. Even if you're simultaneously resizing your HVAC system, you may be able to use and extend existing ductwork.

Some systems use metal ducts while others use flexible heating conduit to run between registers. In either case, here's what you'll do to tie in to existing ductwork:

1. Find a seam or break point in the ductwork where a branch can be installed.

2. Cut the duct and install a joint (available through HVAC suppliers) and the branch duct.

3. Install the register.

HVAC ductwork typically is installed between floors of a house.

Make sure that the ductwork is securely supported.

A suspended ceiling can hide plumbing,
HVAC ducting, and electrical service from view.

Rather than cut floor joists, this ductwork
drops below and around them.

Independent Systems

If your home doesn't have a central heating and
cooling system—or if it does and it's not large
enough to keep the basement comfortable—
consider installing an independent system. An
independent comfort system is one that heats
or cools a single area rather than the entire
house. For example, radiant heat in a bedroom
is an independent system. So is a freestanding
fireplace or a room air conditioner.

Radiant heat systems typically require a specialized contractor or a highly experienced do-
it-yourselfer to install. However, installing a
room air conditioner or plugging in a heater is
easy to do. Just make sure that the unit's capacity is at least 20 percent above the area's heating or cooling requirements.

The Least You Need to Know

◆ Basements require special toilets to over-
come gravity if the main DWV line is
above the toilet.

◆ Plastic and copper pipe and fittings make
installing and extending supply lines and
drain lines relatively easy.

◆ Plumbing fixtures typically are installed
after the walls are closed.

◆ You can either tie in to existing HVAC
systems or install independent systems
depending on basement comfort needs.

In This Chapter

- ◆ Deciding who does the wiring
- ◆ Adding electrical service to your basement
- ◆ Installing fixtures and switches
- ◆ Installing phone, cable, network, and other wire

Chapter **8**

Wiring and Lighting

Your new basement is shaping up. The walls are framed, the plumbing is roughed in, and you're probably anxious to close up the walls and move in. Hold it! You'll need electricity to power life in the basement.

This chapter covers planning and installing electrical wiring and lighting in your basement. It also describes how to install phone, cable, network, intercom, and other wiring systems before the walls are closed up. And it will help you decide whether *you* can do the work yourself or whether you should hire a pro to do it. So let's get started!

D-I-Y or Electrician?

Can you wire your basement's electrical system? Probably. Most local building codes allow homeowners to wire or rewire their own homes. So the question is: *Should* you wire your basement? The answer depends on your understanding of electricity, your skills and experience, how much time you have, and your budget. As you read this chapter you may decide it's a job you'd rather hire someone else to do—or one that you're ready to tackle. Many thousands of homeowners have successfully wired or rewired their homes over the years. You can, too.

Fortunately, most city and county building departments use a common standard for electrical systems. In the United States it's the National Electrical Code (NEC) and in Canada the Canadian Electrical Code (CEC). When you apply for your building permit to finish your basement you will receive more specific information on local electrical and building codes.

Electrical codes make sense. They standardize how electrical systems are installed so that you know what you're getting when you buy a home. They also protect those who eventually buy (or inherit) your home. For example, electrical codes typically require that *receptacles* (plugs) are installed 12 inches from the floor and no more than 12 feet apart. Codes also dictate how wiring and fixtures are installed for safety.

Deeper Meaning _____

A **receptacle** (or outlet) is an electrical device in a wall, ceiling, or floor, into which the plugs on appliance and extension cords are placed to connect them to electric power.

Electrical receptacles or outlets are inexpensive and easy to install.

The next question is: Have you done this kind of work before? Have you installed a main or sub? Have you pulled wire, or set a box, or wired a fixture? No? Not even sure what I'm talking about? No worries, mate. These and related skills will be covered in this chapter.

I'll also show you how to work safely around electricity. That's important to keep you from getting injured. And knowing how to handle electricity without being bit will add to your confidence in working with it.

Adding Electrical Service

Your home is an existing structure. Your unfinished basement, as part of that structure, may or may not already have electrical service readily available to it. So the first step in adding electrical service is figuring out what's needed. If you're working with a designer or a contractor, the work probably has been done and is included in your remodeling plans. Or you may have decided to do it yourself with the help of the NEC code book or software program.

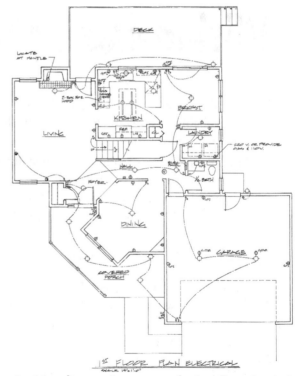

A wiring diagram is your map for installing electrical wiring, switches, receptacles, and fixtures.

Analyzing the Existing System

The first step is figuring out your current electrical system. The place to start the search is at the *service panel*. This is the box or panel where the electricity is distributed to the house circuits. It contains the circuit breakers and, usually, the main disconnect switch. Electrical service comes into your home as 240-volt electricity with two hot (electrified) wires and a neutral wire. Electric ranges and dryers use both hot wires for 240v service. Just about everything else in the home requires 120v service derived from *one* of the hot wires and the neutral wire. The neutral wire also is connected to a grounding system in the service panel, the box where electrical service comes into your home.

Deeper Meaning

A **circuit breaker** is a safety device used to interrupt the flow of power when the electricity exceeds a predetermined amount. Unlike a **fuse**, which you must replace, a circuit breaker can be reset.

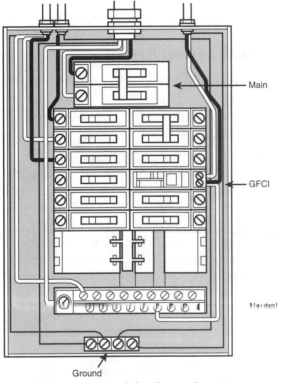

The service panel distributes electricity through circuits, each with its own breaker.

This service panel is surface-mounted on a concrete wall.

The service panel may be part of or attached to the main breaker or fuse panel that distributes the electricity to individual circuits in your home. *Circuit breakers* or *fuses* are the weakest link in the circuit chain, designed to turn off the circuit if there is an overload in it. The breaker can be turned back on or the fuse replaced once the problem is solved.

So your first task is to map the existing electrical system if it hasn't already been done. Professional electricians typically label all the breakers or fuses in the service panel. If not, or if you suspect that a circuit has been added or changed, you can map the existing circuits on paper. Indicate what the circuit controls (bedroom light, kitchen plugs) and their value, in amps, written on the breaker or fuse (15, 20, 30, 40).

Screw-in fuses are found on older homes.

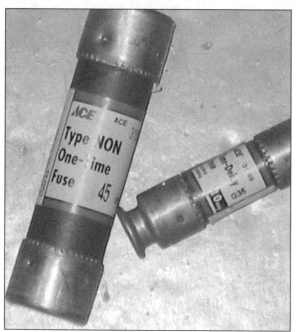

Tube fuses are used for larger amperage circuits in older homes.

Construction Zone

Uncomfortable working around electricity? You *should* be. Electricity can bite. However, if you follow common-sense rules—make sure the circuit is off before working on it, wear rubber-soled shoes, use the correct tools—you should be safe. Take your time and plan the job before doing it. Once done, if you're still uncomfortable, have an electrician show you how to do the job and take a look at it before turning it on.

Calculating Requirements

Why go to all the trouble of mapping the existing electrical system? Because you need to know how much electrical service is available to your basement as well as where existing systems are that you can tap in to.

For example, older homes may be wired for only 100-amp service and expansion will require that the service panel and breaker/fuse panel be updated. Newer homes may be wired for 200-amp service which may not be adequate for finishing the basement. The upgrade should be done by a licensed electrician. However, to determine whether you even need a new service box you must decide how much service you're getting and how much of it is currently being used.

The NEC offers guidelines for service requirements and circuit loads. Basically, make sure that the amps required by all fixtures and appliances (loads) on a circuit don't exceed the circuit's amp rating on the breaker or fuse. If a load is rated in watts rather than amps, divide the watts by 120 (volts). For cxample, a 250-watt appliance draws about 20 amps.

Here are some circuit design tips for your basement:

◆ Make sure the kitchen and laundry room each have at least two 20-amp grounded circuits that are independent of lighting fixtures.

◆ You can install up to eight outlets on a circuit—unless local electrical code says "no."

◆ Install outlets 12 inches above the floor.

◆ Install switches 48 inches above the floor on the swing (door-knob side) of doors.

◆ Install kitchen and bathroom receptacles 8 inches above countertops and 48 inches apart, making sure they are ground-fault circuit interrupters (GFCIs) if near a sink.

◆ Install a separate 15- to 20-amp circuit dedicated to a refrigerator, if planned.

 **On the Level**

Basement remodelers will tell you that it's always better to plan for extra circuits. Installing them now is much cheaper than adding them later.

Installing Subs

If the electrical service to your home is adequate, but you need to add more circuits and breakers, you may be able to add a sub-panel in the basement where it's handy. Actually, unless you've done this before—successfully—consider hiring an electrician to install a sub-panel for you. The sub-panel simply takes some of the electrical service from the main or service panel and routes it to a central location where it can be split into new circuits.

From the main panel or sub-panel you can install a circuit breaker, run wiring to the fixture, and install the receptacle or fixture. These topics will be covered next.

Smaller sub-panels serve fewer circuits than the main panel.

Typical electrical breaker.

Breakers are installed in a sub-panel by removing knock-outs that cover the hole.

Running Wire

Wire size is indicated by its gauge. The smaller the gauge number the larger the wire, and the more electrical current it can carry. Common electrical cable for residential use is labeled *Type NM 12-2 G* meaning it has a nonmetallic (plastic) sheathing covering two 12-gauge wires plus a ground wire (bare).

Reading Cable

Wire cable typically has numbers on the insulation that tell you what's inside. 10-2 cable includes two 10-gauge wires. One wire is black (hot) and the other is white (neutral). 10-3 cable adds a red (hot) wire for 240-volt service such as electric dryers and stoves. Remember: *Always* connect the same colors together (black to black, etc.). *Never* connect black to white or to other color wire.

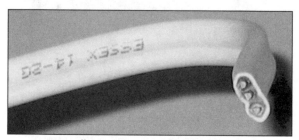

Nonmetallic (NM) wire includes two or more insulated wires and possibly one bare ground wire.

Installing wire cable between an electrical box and the service panel is called pulling cable. You install switch and fixture boxes where they need to be, then drill holes in studs along the most direct path to the service panel. Cables for lights and switches run higher in the wall and in the ceiling; cables for receptacles run low in the walls. Once you cut the length at the panel, mark the cable to indicate what it goes to. Then "make up" the service panel by attaching the individual circuits to breakers.

Once the cables are in place, remove any slack and (carefully) staple the cable to wall framing so that it doesn't move around. Your electrical plans and building department can tell you how frequently staples are needed (typically, every 4½ feet and within 12 inches of the electrical box).

Note that the building inspector will want to take a look at your handy work twice, once when the wire cable is run to the fixtures and once after the fixtures are installed.

In many basements, the exterior walls are concrete or masonry block, making wiring difficult. Unless you install a false wall over the solid wall you're going to have to run all wiring and install fixtures on the outside of the wall. Fortunately, there are materials and wires for doing just that. They include channels, corners, covers, and special switches and fixtures that are mounted on the wall rather than in it. If required, larger building material and electrical suppliers will have the components and installation instructions.

Alternatively, you may need to run wire in a basement wall that is already closed. This job is more time-consuming because you insert a "fish line" or stiff wire with a hook on the end into the wall and run it all the way to the service box. The best place to start is at the hole you make for the fixture or receptacle and fish it toward the service box. Obviously, you can't cut holes in any wall studs that stand in the way so you may need to be creative in how you use the fish line. Once you get it to the service box, connect the wire cable to the fish line and pull it through.

Installing Fixtures and Switches

Residential wiring is so common that the cable, fixtures, and methods are standardized. You can buy standard fixture and receptacle boxes at most hardware stores. However, it's best to buy them from an electrical store or department where a knowledgeable clerk can help you select the right ones for the job. Find a clerk who can explain installation and offer tips from his or her own experience. You may pay a little more, but you'll get value.

Electrical boxes are attached to studs in the wall, then the wire is run.

NM (nonmetallic) cable is run from the box to the electrical panel.

Fixtures are wired from and attached to the box

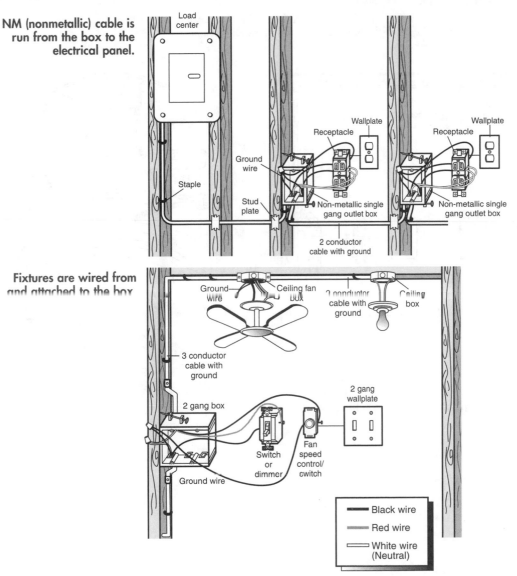

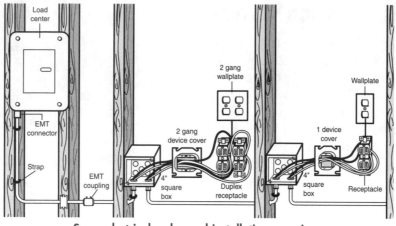

Some electrical codes and installations require that the wires be housed in metal conduit.

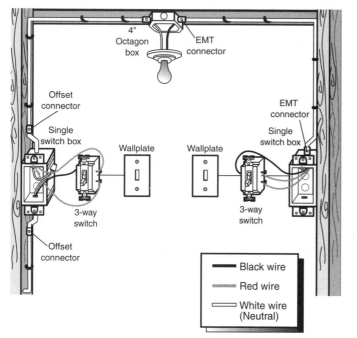

Black wire

Red wire

White wire
(Neutral)

Metal conduit typically requires metal boxes.

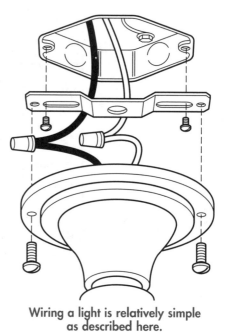

Wiring a light is relatively simple as described here.

**Electrical receptacles and switches require
a cover to protect people from shock.**

The tools needed for installing fixtures, switches, and receptacles are basic. They include a cable stripper, wire stripper, needle-nose pliers, and a circuit tester. Here's the process:

1. Make sure that power to the circuit is off.
2. Cut the wire cable to a length 6 to 8 inches beyond the front of the box.
3. Remove sheathing from the wire cable inside the box.
4. Strip the last inch of sheathing from the end of each covered wire.
5. Connect the ground (bare or green) wire to the receptacle, fixture, switch, or box.
6. Connect the white (neutral) wire to the receptacle, fixture, or switch.
7. Connect the black (hot) wire to the receptacle, fixture, or switch.
8. Mount the receptacle, fixture, or switch on the box.

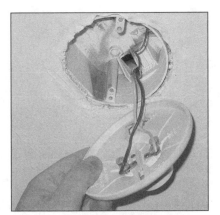

Attach the wires using electrical nuts.

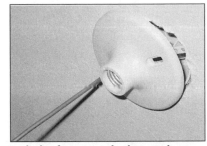

Attach the fixture to the box with screws.

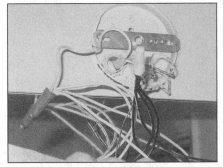

Some light fixtures have multiple connections.

Some fixtures are more challenging to wire. For example, installing a fan-with-light unit will have additional wiring. Also, a fixture that can be turned off by two or more switches will need to be wired differently. Fortunately, the fixtures typically come with a connection diagram.

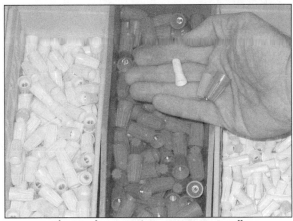

**Electrical connection nuts come in all
shapes, sizes, and colors.**

Note that there are special lighting fixtures for suspended ceilings (see Chapter 9). The fixture will include installation procedures.

Wiring Switches and Receptacles

Wiring your basement for electricity is relatively easy—once you have an electrical plan. It shows what fixtures, switches, and receptacles go where. Here are some guidelines to help you install switches and receptacles yourself.

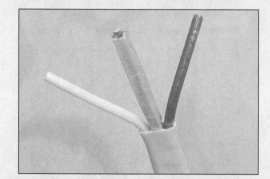

Interior home wiring typically is Type 12-2 w/G, meaning two 12-gauge wires (black is hot, white is neutral), and a ground wire.

In addition to 12-2 w/G (left), some installations require 14-3 w/G (right), meaning two 14-gauge (smaller than 12-gauge) with a ground wire.

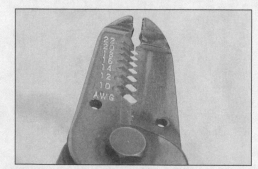

Wire strippers have holes designed to strip specific gauge wire, from 10 (larger) to 22 (smaller) AWG (American Wire Gauge) sizes.

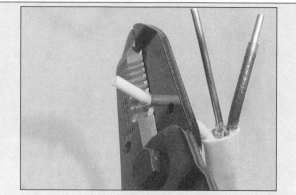

Insulation is stripped (removed) from the end of wires by clamping the wire in the appropriate size opening of the stripper to cut the wire, then pulling to remove the sheathing. Ground wires typically are wrapped in a paper that can easily be removed by hand.

Electrical boxes can be nailed or screwed to studs. Soft areas at the rear of the box, called punch-outs, can be removed to run wires in and out of the box as needed. Switches and receptacles are attached to the box using the top and bottom screw holes.

Wires can be attached to a switch either at terminals or in holes on the back of the switch. To release the wire, insert a flat screwdriver into the slot next to the hole. Some switches also have a strip gauge on the back to show you how much insulation should be removed from a wire before installation.

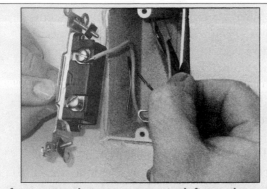

If connecting the wire to a terminal, first make a curl in the end so it wraps around the terminal clockwise.

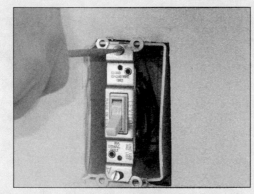

Two screws attach the switch to the terminal box. The oversize hole allows for side-to-side adjustment of the switch within the box to make it straight.

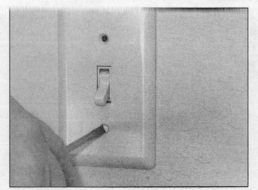

Finally, install the switch cover. Make sure the switch is in the off position before turning the circuit on at the electrical service panel.

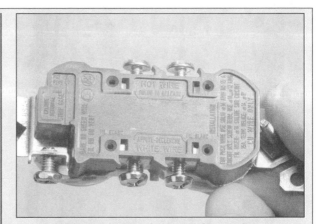

Receptacles (outlets or plugs), too, have either terminals, holes, or both. Note that the hot (black or red) wires are attached to one side of the terminal and the white (neutral) wire to the other side. The second set of hot and neutral screws are for continuing power on to another plug. The fifth screw is for the ground wire.

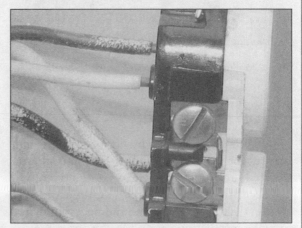

In this case, electrical wires were inserted into the connection holes of the outlet rather than attached to the side terminal screws. (Note: The white paint on the wires is overspray from the painters, not snow.)

Make sure wall lights are sufficiently high to illuminate pictures and reading areas.

Installing Other Wire

Hey, while you're at it, why not install wire and fixtures for your telephone, television, computer, stereo, home entertainment system, intercom, and security system? Before the walls are covered in drywall, you can run the necessary wires to make installation easier. Or you can run a plastic pipe or conduit through the walls that you can use to install low-voltage wiring (phone, cable, audio) in the future. Just make sure you map out where it goes and where the junction boxes are so you can easily access them later.

Numerous security components are available at larger hardware stores.

What's required to install these systems now? Design and planning. That is, decide where you want telephone jacks, TV cable, computer network connections, and security sensors. Then select the jacks or receptacles and wiring needed to connect the devices at a Radio Shack or other electronics parts store. Run the wire and install any needed boxes before finishing the walls, then install the receptacles once the walls are done. Because these systems carry relatively low voltage (5 volts or less), safety is not much of an issue so inspection may not be required.

Hardware stores typically carry dozens of phone plugs, wires, and tools for the do-it-yourselfer.

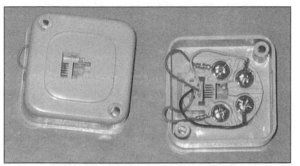

Once wired, this phone plug is mounted
on a wall or baseboard.

Smaller wiring (larger gauge number) is used
for wiring phones, security, sound, and other
systems in your basement.

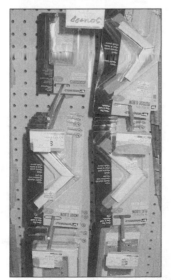

You can install wire on wall and baseboard surfaces
using various surface wiring components available
at larger hardware stores.

Alternatively, new technology offers wireless remote operation and communication for telephones, computer networks, and even security equipment. So if installing wire for these systems isn't relatively easy, think outside the wall.

The Least You Need to Know

◆ Do-it-yourselfers can tackle most of the wiring and lighting jobs needed for finishing a basement.

◆ Analyze your current electrical system then calculate what the finished basement will require to determine if you need to add a sub-panel or install a new service panel.

◆ Even if you hire an electrician for the technical work, you can save money by running wire and installing fixtures and switches in your basement.

◆ While the walls are open, consider what other systems you can wire and install right now.

In This Chapter

- ◆ Exploring your ceiling options

- ◆ Planning to close up your basement's ceiling

- ◆ Making sure that all electrical and comfort systems are installed

- ◆ Installing popular types of ceilings

    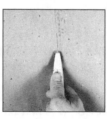

Finishing Ceilings

You've installed all the wiring and plumbing in the walls and ceiling. And your handiwork has passed inspection. Great! What's next?

Your basement will start looking more like a residence now as you "close up" or install the ceiling, wall, and flooring. This chapter covers the first step, finishing ceilings. (Most builders and remodelers start at the top of the room and work down, depending on the type of ceiling to be installed.)

Ceiling Systems

A ceiling is the interior sheathing or covering of an overhead surface. You have many options here, though they could be limited by the height available in the basement.

As discussed in Chapter 2, building codes typically require that the height of a room (floor to ceiling) must be at least 7 feet 6 inches. An exception is made under most building codes for beams under the main floor (the basement's ceiling). If the beams are at least 4 feet apart the space below them can be 7 feet. There are other exceptions to ceiling height requirements as well so make sure you know local building requirements.

So your decision as to what ceiling system you'll install depends on what space you have available. A suspended ceiling, for example, may drop the ceiling's height by 6 inches or more. Let's consider the options.

For many basements, an unfinished ceiling is just fine. The floor *joists* for the floor above are overhead and exposed. Wiring and HVAC ducts are visible. Finishing may require only a thorough cleaning, fastening wires more securely, and maybe painting or finishing the joists. After all, it's a basement.

The more popular option is to finish the basement ceiling similar to the ceilings throughout the house. That means installing a drywall, tile, or suspended ceiling.

Drywall is a popular building material that has virtually replaced lath (wood strips) and plaster as the preferred ceiling and wall finish. The primary reason is because it's easier to install, making it ideal for do-it-yourselfers. Drywall is an engineered building panel made from gypsum and other materials in a kraft paper cover. Drywall is also called gypsum, wallboard, plasterboard, or by various brand names such as Sheetrock.

Ceiling tiles are squares attached to wood strips installed across floor joists. The tiles typically are 1 foot square. Besides being more soundproof than drywall, they are even easier for do-it-yourselfers to install. You'll learn how later in this chapter.

A suspended ceiling is a system for installing ceiling tile by hanging a metal framework from the ceiling (or higher floor) joists. The tiles, too, are relatively easy to install. Their primary advantage is that they allow access to the floor joists, wiring, and HVAC systems above. A tile can be lifted out of the frame and moved aside for access.

There's one more point to consider as you plan and install your basement's ceiling: *soffits*. A soffit is any horizontal surface attached to but below the ceiling. Cabinets that don't go all the way to the ceiling, for example, are often hung from soffits. The great thing about soffits is that they can hide things such as overhead pipe, as you saw in Chapter 6. If HVAC ductwork is below the bottom of the joists, it can be enclosed in a soffit and the ceiling attached to

the joists. If you're using an architect's plans or a remodeling software program, the soffits are probably already in the plan. However, if you're planning as you go, remember to plan for building and covering soffits.

Before Closing the Ceiling

Before installing the ceiling—even if it's a suspended ceiling—make sure that all wiring and HVAC ductwork is completed. In addition, inspect existing wiring and ductwork for condition. It will be easier to repair or replace it now than later.

The area around the floor joists may be the best or only location for new wiring (see Chapter 8) and new plumbing (see Chapter 7). Make sure that you're not permanently sealing them away from repair. Don't hide electrical junction boxes or plumbing shutoffs behind the ceiling. Instead, plan for and install an access panel in the ceiling. It can be a framed door or simply a tile or two that can easily be moved for access to components above.

Make sure everything is in place in the ceiling before closing it up.

Finally, install insulation and soundproofing following your building plans. I'll show you how in Chapter 10.

Installing Ceilings

Time to quit planning and get to work! In this section, you'll learn how to install drywall ceilings, ceiling tiles, and suspended ceilings.

Note that drywall ceilings typically are installed *before*, but tile and suspended ceilings are usually installed *after*, walls are covered. So you may need to read Chapter 10 before continuing. Also, lighting and other fixtures are installed (see Chapter 8) after the ceiling is installed.

Installing Drywall Ceilings

Drywall is available in sheets of 4 by 8 feet or 4 by 12 feet. The 12-feet length is for larger rooms and are not very easy to install so the 8-feet length is preferred by do-it-yourselfers. Drywall comes in thicknesses of ¼ to ¾ inch. To keep ceilings from sagging, ½ and ⅝ inch are preferred. The only disadvantages to the thicker sheets is their additional weight and price.

Drywall is sold in assorted thicknesses and for various applications.

Drywall is available in various lengths.

When selecting drywall, consider its use. If it's being installed in an area prone to produce moisture such as a bathroom, make sure you get water-resistant drywall. It's usually blue or green in color—and more expensive.

How Much Drywall Will You Need?

To determine how much drywall you'll need to buy, measure the ceiling to find its square footage and add 20 percent for waste, then divide the total by 32. There are 32 square feet in a 4-by-8-feet sheet of drywall. For example, if the combined ceilings in your basement are 400 square feet, add 80 square feet for waste for a total of 480 square feet Divide it by 32 and you come up with 15 sheets of 4-by-8-feet drywall. Note that experienced drywallers add just 10 percent, but they are often very creative in using scrap.

Drywall is installed on ceilings by two people or by one person with a drywall lift that you can rent at larger rental stores. Sheets are installed lengthwise across the joists starting in one corner of the room. Measure the joists and cut the board if needed to ensure that it ends at the center of a joist. Attach the sheets to the joists with drywall nails or screws placed every 8 inches around the sheet's perimeter and every 12 inches into other joists. The local building code will tell you local requirements for installing drywall fasteners.

On the Level _____

The long edges of drywall sheets are tapered so the seam can be filled and smoothed later. If possible, always orient the sheets on the ceiling (or wall) in the same direction so the tapered edges abut.

Cutting drywall is relatively easy because it is simply gypsum wrapped in paper. Place the board across sawhorses, measure, and use a ruler or straightedge to indicate where the sheet should be cut. Use a drywall, utility, or similar knife to cut into but not through the drywall. Bend the board to make it break at the score and cut the opposite side. If needed, use a sanding block to rub the edge flat for fitting.

Drywall is simply gypsum plaster sandwiched between heavy papers.

Mark the cut.

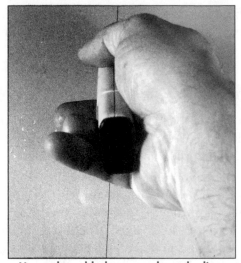

Use a sharp blade to cut along the line.

Break the drywall along the cut.

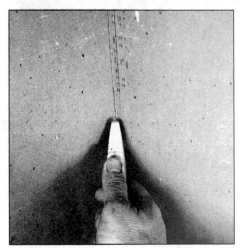

Cut the paper on the back side of the break.

As needed, carefully sand the edge.

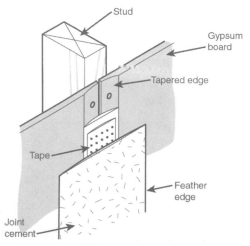

Layers of filling a drywall joint.

Drywall sheets are staggered on the ceiling. That is, the first row starts with a full 8-foot-wide sheet and the second row starts with a half-sheet that's 4-foot wide. That keeps the next row of drywall sheet joints 4 feet apart.

You'll be cutting holes in the ceiling drywall later for lighting fixtures, so mark their location as you install the sheets. Alternatively, you can cut the needed holes as you install the drywall to ensure accuracy.

The next job is to cover the joints between sheets, called taping. Apply a thin layer of drywall compound to cover the seams, then apply drywall tape along the seam and let it dry. Then use a wide wallboard or putty knife to apply and thinly spread additional drywall compound. Once dry, carefully sand the surface smooth so that the seam doesn't show. Of course, the easiest time to tape ceiling drywall is at the same time you're taping wall drywall (see Chapter 10). Make sure you fill in the nail or screw holes at the same time.

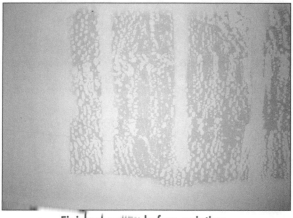

Finished ceiling before painting.

Finally, if you want to add texture to the ceiling, take a look at the various ceiling texture products available at larger building material and paint stores. Some are for the pros, but newer products can be installed by the do-it-yourselfer.

Installing Ceiling Tile

Ceiling tiles are relatively easy to install. All you need are the interlocking tiles, a stapler or glue cartridge, a saw, and a flat surface. The ceiling surface can be furring (strips of wood spaced the width of the tile), drywall, or plywood.

Standard acoustic ceiling tile has lips on all four sides, but the lips on two sides are larger. Make sure you install them with the larger lips facing you, as shown.

Once the first tile is in place, use a shop stapler to fasten the tile to the surface, attaching in at least two places per side.

Staple through the other large lip in at least two places. If the tip of the staple isn't below the lip surface, use a nail set to lower it.

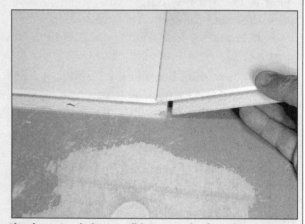

Slip the second tile's small lips in to the first tile, as shown.

Staple the large lips on the second tile.

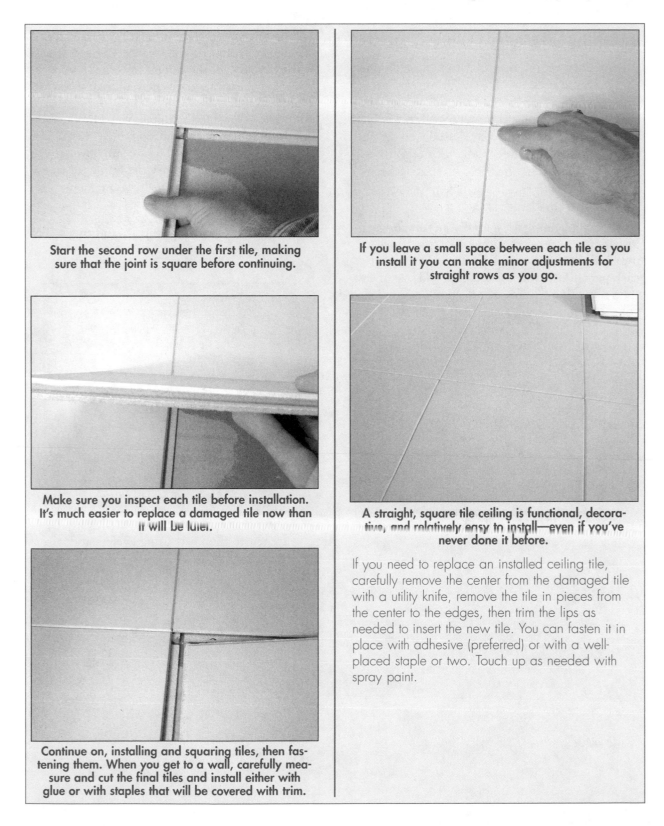

Start the second row under the first tile, making sure that the joint is square before continuing.

Make sure you inspect each tile before installation. It's much easier to replace a damaged tile now than it will be later.

Continue on, installing and squaring tiles, then fastening them. When you get to a wall, carefully measure and cut the final tiles and install either with glue or with staples that will be covered with trim.

If you leave a small space between each tile as you install it you can make minor adjustments for straight rows as you go.

A straight, square tile ceiling is functional, decorative, and relatively easy to install—even if you've never done it before.

If you need to replace an installed ceiling tile, carefully remove the center from the damaged tile with a utility knife, remove the tile in pieces from the center to the edges, then trim the lips as needed to insert the new tile. You can fasten it in place with adhesive (preferred) or with a well-placed staple or two. Touch up as needed with spray paint.

Installing Suspended Ceilings

A suspended ceiling is similar to a tile ceiling in that both use tiles on a frame. However, a tile ceiling is nailed to a frame of furring strips while a suspended ceiling uses a metal grid that is hung or suspended from the joists. Suspended ceiling tiles are available in 2-feet squares, and 2-by-4-feet rectangles. The smaller ones have less tendency to sag with age, but will require more framing than the larger size.

Careful planning is especially important when installing a suspended ceiling. Use grid paper to measure the room and plan out the location of each panel. Also note the location and size of any special lighting fixtures that need to be installed in your suspended ceiling (see Chapter 8).

You can install a suspended lighting panel in a drywall ceiling as well.

The first step toward installing a suspended ceiling is establishing the location of the frame. Because you want the ceiling to be level, you will mark the location on the wall then make additional wall marks around the room at a point that is level to the initial mark. Remember that code will require headroom of at least 7 feet 6 inches. In addition, make sure you have at least 3 inches of space above the frame for room to install the tiles. Here are the subsequent steps:

1. Install the wall molding around the perimeter walls.

Install the wall molding first.

2. Install the main runners parallel and fastened to the joists using eyelets and wire for support.

Fasten the frame.

3. Attach the individual cross tees into the wall molding and main runners.

Attach the cross tees.

4. Install the panels by lifting them through the openings at an angle and lowering them into place on the frame.

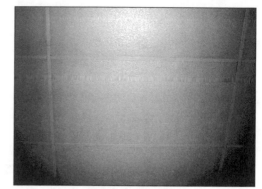

Install the panels.

 **On the Level**

The easiest way to install a frame hanger is to install the upper clip and attach the hanging wire, then insert the wire into the frame and make sure it's level before bending and twisting the lower end of the wire. Most hangers are simply bare 18-gauge wire.

The Least You Need to Know

◆ Make sure that you've done all the electrical and HVAC work needed before closing up the ceiling.

◆ Drywall is the most popular ceiling and wall sheathing, but it isn't the easiest to install.

◆ Be sure that your new ceiling offers at least 7 feet 6 inches of headroom in your basement, depending on local building codes.

◆ Ceiling tiles can be installed on joists using furring strips.

◆ A suspended ceiling is not only easy to install, but also can incorporate lighting fixtures.

In This Chapter

◆ Understanding basement wall systems

◆ Insulating and soundproofing walls

◆ Installing drywall and paneling

◆ Finishing the room with trim

Finishing Walls

It's amazing how quickly an open space can begin looking like a room once the walls are installed and finished. It's like magic!

This chapter shows you how to close in or finish walls after the wiring and plumbing are installed. It will also guide you in selecting and installing insulation to cut energy costs.

First, take a moment to congratulate yourself on the progress you've made toward finishing your basement. Okay, now get back to work!

Wall Systems

A wall is a vertical divider. It separates the inside from the outside or one room from another. It also supports the ceiling and any subsequent walls and ceilings above. Basement perimeter walls also serve as the house's foundation so they are especially sturdy—but not very attractive. Nor are the open wood frame walls with plumbing and wiring inside. Wall sheathing offers a smooth, flat surface for painting, hanging things, and a backdrop for your furnishings.

Walls separate rooms and make the basement look more finished.

Kitchens can offer a challenge to drywall installation.

Basement posts also are a challenge to drywall.

Finished drywall gives the room an inviting look.

Selecting Drywall

Which size and thickness of drywall should you use? Most do-it-yourselfers prefer 4-by-8-feet sheets over larger ones because they're easier to handle. Drywall that is ⅜-inch thick is preferred for installation over wood wall framing and ¼-inch drywall if you're installing over old drywall or paneling. Ceilings will sag if the drywall is too thin, so ⅝-inch drywall is preferred there.

Paneling is sold in 4-by-8-foot sheets, finished and ready to hang.

Drywall is the most popular wall sheathing today. Before that it was lath and plaster—lath, or strips of wood, were nailed to the studs then covered with plaster that was smoothed out by hand before it dried. Next on the popularity list is prefinished paneling that can be attached to the wall framing or to sheets of drywall.

If attaching drywall or prefinished paneling to an exterior concrete wall, first install 1-by-2-inch wood strips (furring strips). They support the sheathing and offer something to attach it to. Furring strips can be glued to the concrete or installed with special concrete nails available through building suppliers.

As with ceilings, consider installing access panels in your basement's walls to allow access to sewer line cleanouts, electrical service boxes, and HVAC equipment. Don't drywall over them and later try to figure out where they are. Simply build a small door or other opening in the sheathing for future access. You can also use built-in cabinets as wall components, especially for shorter walls.

Unique built-in pantry.

The pantry swings out to offer storage behind.

Selecting Insulation

Insulation simply slows down the heat transfer process. There are many popular types of insulation including:

- ◆ Flexible insulation
- ◆ Loose-fill insulation
- ◆ Reflective insulation
- ◆ Rigid insulation
- ◆ Everything else

Deeper Meaning

Insulation is any material that resists the conduction of heat, sound, or electricity.

Let's take a closer look at each category.

Flexible Insulation

You've seen rolls of flexible insulation before. Typically, it's made of fiberglass or a similar fiber. It comes in two types: batt and blanket.

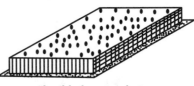

Flexible batt insulation.

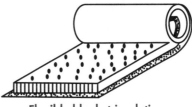

Flexible blanket insulation.

Batt insulation is made of fibrous material in thicknesses of 4 and 6 inches for 16- and 24-inch joist spacing. It is supplied with or without a vapor barrier. Friction batts are supplied without a covering and will remain in place without staples.

Blanket insulation comes in rolls or packages in widths suited to 16- and 24-inch stud and joist spacing. The body of the blanket is made of felted mats of mineral or vegetable fibers such as rock or glass wool, wood fiber, and cotton. Organic insulations are treated to make them resistant to fire, decay, insects, and vermin.

Most blanket insulation is covered with paper or other sheet material and has tabs on the sides for fastening to studs or joists. One covering sheet serves as a vapor barrier to resist water vapor. It should always face the warm side of the wall. Aluminum foil, asphalt, or plastic-laminated paper are commonly used as exterior barrier materials.

Loose-Fill Insulation

Loose-fill insulation comes in bags or bales, and is placed by poring, blowing, or packing by hand. It includes rock or glass wool, wood fibers, shredded redwood bark, cork, wood pulp products, vermiculite, sawdust, and shavings. It is more popular in attics than in basements.

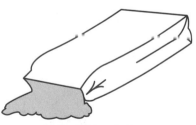

Loose-fill insulation.

Reflective Insulation

Most materials reflect some radiant heat, and some materials do so more than others. The more reflective materials include aluminum foil, sheet metal with tin coating, and paper products coated with a reflective oxide.

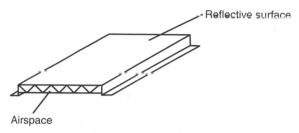

Reflective insulation.

Reflective insulation is used in enclosed stud spaces, attics, and similar place to retard the transfer of radiated heat. They are effective only when used where the reflective surface faces an airspace at least ¾ inch or more deep. Foil-type reflective insulation is often applied to insulation blankets.

Rigid Insulation

Rigid insulation is usually a fiberboard material manufactured in sheets. Structural insulating boards range in densities from 15 to 31 pounds per cubic foot and are fabricated into building boards, roof decking, sheathing, and wallboard. While they have moderately good insulating properties, their primary purpose is structural.

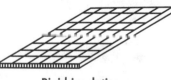

Rigid insulation.

The most common forms of rigid insulation is sheathing board in ½-inch and $^{25}/_{32}$-inch thicknesses. It is coated or impregnated with an asphalt or other compound to provide water resistance. Sheets are 2 feet by 8 feet for horizontal installation and 4 feet by 8 feet or longer for vertical applications.

Installing and Taping Drywall

Hanging drywall doesn't require a lot of skill—just a helper lifting the panels to the wall or ceiling for fastening. However, some folks decide to hire a professional drywall taper to install the seams. Not necessary. If you're adventuresome—and start in a room that's not as conspicuous—you can teach yourself to tape like a pro. Here's how it's done.

Cutting drywall is relatively easy. Use a straight-edge to score and cut one side, typically the front, then bend the board at the score and cut the paper on the back, as shown.

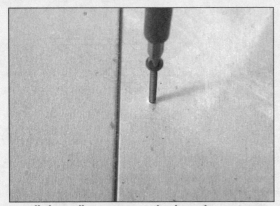

Install drywall screws or nails along the perimeter of the sheet at 6- to 12-inch intervals, depending on local building code.

A wide drywall knife, shown, spans the tapered edges of two butted sheets. Also known as a broad-knife, this one is 10 inches wide and costs less than $6.00 at a local hardware store.

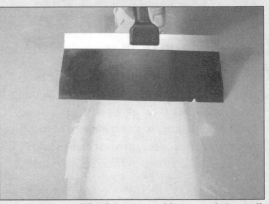

Use the drywall knife to smoothly spread drywall joint compound (also called mud) across the joint.

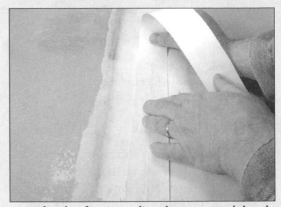

Immediately after spreading the compound, lay the joint tape (typically 2 inches) along the joint.

Joint tape has a middle crease to match to the joint, making it easier to center.

Fill the dimple with joint compound using a drywall knife.

Finally, apply more joint compound over the tape for a smooth joint. Once dry, sand the joint with a large sandpaper block.

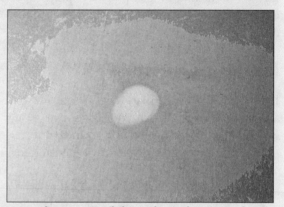

Once the compound dries, the nail or screw head will not be detectable. Sand and paint.

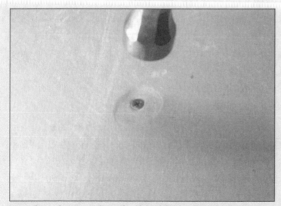

Nail and screw heads should be dimpled with a hammer to make sure they are lower than the drywall surface.

Other Insulating Stuff

There are other energy-efficient home insulation materials available, with new ones coming out all the time. They include insulation blankets made of multiple layers of corrugated paper.

Other materials are formed-in-place insulations, which include sprayed and plastic types. Sprayed insulation is usually inorganic fibrous material blown against a clean surface that has been primed with an adhesive coating.

Foams can be molded or sprayed in place. Urethane insulation is applied by spraying. Polystyrene and urethane boards are available in ½-inch to 2-inch thicknesses.

Installing Insulation

Insulation should be placed on all outside walls and in the floor joists of your basement. You can also install insulation as a soundproofing material in interior walls. How is it installed?

- Install flexible blanket or batt insulation between wall studs and staple in place.
- Install flexible blanket or batt insulation between floor joists and support with slats, wire, staples, or held in place by friction and the ceiling.
- Install a vapor barrier on exterior walls.
- Install rigid insulation inside exterior walls with adhesive.

Installing Drywall

Drywall is still the most popular wall sheathing material today. It's relatively easy to install, though many do-it-yourselfers opt to hire someone to come in and tape it for them. Taping is a developed skill that requires either experience or practice in an unseen corner of your basement.

Selecting Drywall

I introduced drywall in Chapter 9. To summarize, drywall is an engineered building panel made from gypsum and other materials in a paper cover. It's also called gypsum, wallboard, plasterboard, or Sheetrock.

Drywall comes in 4 feet wide sheets in lengths of 8, 12, and 16 feet, however the shorter lengths are preferred by do-it-yourselfers because of the weight and difficulty in handling longer lengths. Preferred thickness for walls is ½ inches. Also available are ⅜ inch (to cut costs) and ⅝ inch (for additional support).

Mounting Drywall

If you've already installed drywall on the basement's ceiling (as in Chapter 9), installing it on the walls will be relatively easy. The widest part of the first sheets are butted to the ceiling then attached to studs with drywall nails or screws. Once the top course is done, measure the lower section of the wall to within ¼ inch of the floor and cut a sheet to fit.

If you're installing a suspended or tile ceiling the walls go up before the ceiling. Butt the sheets up to the joists and attach them to studs with drywall nails or screws. Then cut and install the lower course of drywall. Finally, install the ceiling system.

Cut drywall.

Drywall sheets are staggered on the wall. The first row starts with a full 8-foot wide sheet and the second row starts with a half sheet, 4-foot wide, to keep the drywall sheet joints on the next row 4 feet apart.

 On the Level

Professional drywall installers set the sheet in place against a wall, then insert a wedge and fulcrum below the bottom edge to lift and adjust the sheet with foot pressure before nailing. Once the sheet is against the framing it is difficult to move and adjust otherwise.

Installing Doors and Windows

Installing doors and windows was covered in Chapter 6. However, their installation actually comes after the walls are finished, so here's a pictorial review of the components and process.

Prehung door.

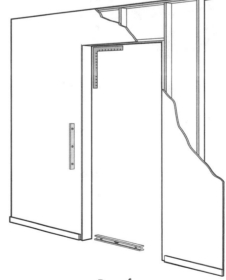

Door frame.

Doorjamb.

Installed door.

Installing a prehung door.

Installing Paneling

Instead of installing drywall, many homeowners use paneling to sheath their new basement walls. There are two types of paneling products available. The most popular is a laminate that comes in 4-by-8-feet sheets with a decorative design on one side. The other type is wood or laminate tongue-and-groove strips that interlock to form the wall surface. Typically, panels are easier and faster to install than drywall.

Remember to acclimate the panels before installation. That is, bring them into the basement and let them come to room temperature and humidity.

Depending on the surface on which you're installing them, panels can be fastened with nails or adhesive. If you use nails, select finish nails of the same approximate color as the panel so the nail heads blend in. Alternatively, you can fill the nail holes later with a colored filler. Drive the nails into the studs about every 8 inches.

Adhesive is applied on studs or directly on a masonry wall, then the panel is placed in position and pressed. Use a heavy roller to seal the panel to the adhesive.

If you need to cut a panel, do so with a power saw *finish side down*. If cutting with a hand saw, keep the *finish side up*. These methods will minimize damage to the finish.

On the Level

To mark the location of fixtures that need panel cutouts, mark the perimeter of the fixture with lipstick or a grease pencil and press the panel in place.

Installing Trim

Once the walls are in place it's time to consider the trim. Though decorative, most wall base trim is also functional. It keeps furniture and other objects from damaging the wall. It also covers rough edges of the wall sheathing.

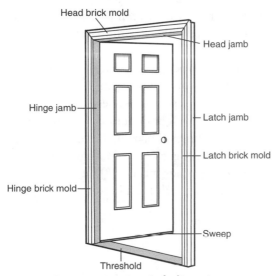

Door components including trim.

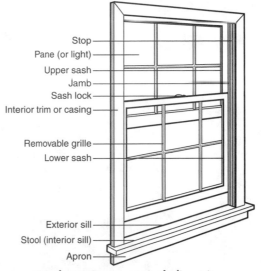

Window components including trim.

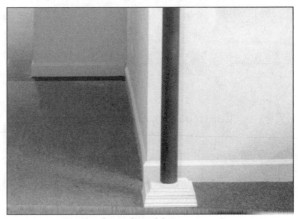

Baseboard and lamp trim.

Depending on your basement's design you may want to install trim after the walls are finished *or* after the flooring is done. For example, install the baseboard now if you're installing carpeting, but hold off until after a tile or other hard floor is installed. Door trim can be installed at the same time as baseboards. Window trim can be installed at any time after the wall is finished and the window is installed.

A wide variety of trim is used in this basement.

Construction Zone

Consider painting the walls *before* installing the trim. The most difficult part of painting is working around the trim once it's installed.

You can purchase trim molding at most building material stores.

A baseboard is the horizontal trim at the joint of the wall and floor. Door and window trim cover the gap between the frame and the wall. Fortunately, these trim materials are readily available in building material and lumber stores so the trick to installation is cutting them to fit. Because most trim joints are cut at an angle, a miter saw is the best tool. Fancy cutting requires a compound miter saw that can cut two angles (horizontal *and* vertical) at once. Most trim is cut at a 45 degree angle; two pieces together make a 90 degree turn. Sand the cut smooth for a better fit.

A basement entertainment center is set off with trim.

**Even an alcove below the stairs
can benefit from trim.**

Install trim with finish nails at least twice as long as the wood is thick. Nail in to sill plates, studs, and other large wood members rather than just into the drywall.

Drywall, paneling, and finish nails.

The Least You Need to Know

◆ Wall sheathing is installed before tile or suspended ceilings and after drywall ceilings.

◆ Insulation can not only reduce heating bills, it can also serve as soundproofing between rooms in your new basement.

◆ Plan out your drywall installation on paper to save time and waste.

◆ Paneling typically is easier to install than drywall, making it popular with do-it-yourselfers.

◆ Trim both protects and adds a decorative touch to walls.

In This Chapter

- ◆ Exploring your flooring options
- ◆ Getting your basement ready for flooring
- ◆ Prepping the subfloor
- ◆ Installing various types of flooring
- ◆ Putting the finishing touches on your basement floor

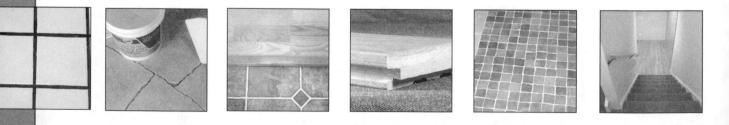

Chapter 11

Remodeling Floors

By now your basement is beginning to look livable. It's plumbed and wired and enclosed. Now comes the flooring.

This chapter shows you how to install your own flooring—or hire the right person to do the work. It covers hardwood, laminate wood, sheet and square vinyl tile, and carpet. It even shows you how to paint a concrete basement floor. Finally, you'll learn how to finish your basement's new floor.

Planning the Flooring

Installing flooring is relatively easy, depending on what you select and the condition of the basement subfloor. For example, interlocking laminate wood flooring, called a floating floor, can be installed in hours—once the prep work is done. A hardwood floor will take longer.

So the first step in installing basement flooring is to prepare the subfloor. I'll cover that in the next section. Meantime, consider what you're working with, what materials you prefer, how easy it is to install it yourself, and how to buy it.

Most unfinished basements have a subfloor of concrete that's below grade and subject to moisture. Fortunately, you've taken care of the moisture problems (see Chapter 6). However, most new flooring will require additional prep in the form of a moisture barrier above the subfloor. So as you consider and shop for flooring, think about the basement's subfloor and what it will take to get it ready for the chosen flooring material. You'll find lots of options including various barriers that can easily be installed over the existing subfloor and below your new flooring.

Sizing

How much flooring will you need? Now that your basement is broken up into rooms, you'll need to get an exact measurement so you can start shopping for flooring materials.

To calculate the room's size, simply multiply the width times the length. A 10-feet-by-12-feet room has 120 square feet of floor. It would be wonderful if all rooms were square or rectangular. However, many rooms include closets, doorways, alcoves, and other mathematical challenges. Fortunately, most of them are made up of rectangles. By measuring each rectangle and adding the results to the other rectangles, you can come up with the total square feet for flooring.

Hold on. There's waste. Depending on the type of flooring material you select, the shape of rooms, and your own skills, add 10 to 20 percent to the total as the waste factor. Frankly, 10 percent is usually adequate even for the first time do-it-yourselfer *if* he or she plans the job and takes time to prep and install it. Also, lower quality flooring materials may have more culls or bad pieces that shouldn't be installed. In fact, some manufacturers suggest you allow up to 5 percent for culls.

Materials

What materials should you select for flooring? Much depends on budget and taste. Sheet and square vinyl typically is the least expensive, carpeting is in the middle of the expense chart, solid hardwood is near the top, and ceramic tile is usually the most costly. Of course, the final price depends on the quality as well as how and where you buy it.

Also consider the cost—or savings—of installation. Get a quote from the flooring or building material store on what it will cost to have a professional installer do the work. It can be from $3 to $6 or more per square foot. Add this to the total cost if you're hiring someone to install it—or consider it savings if you do it yourself. I'll show you how to install flooring later in this chapter.

How Easy Is It to Install?

You may decide to install flooring yourself. If so, ease of installation becomes more important. The easiest to install typically is self-adhesive vinyl tile and interlocking laminate wood products. In fact, they are sold primarily to do-it-yourselfers because most pros don't use cheaper tile or laminates. Carpeting is relatively easy to install if you rent and learn to use seamers and stretchers. Installing solid wood flooring can take more time, but the results can be beautiful—especially if you buy some of the new prefinished materials that don't require subsequent sanding and finishing. Ceramic and porcelain tile is more difficult to install, but thousands of do-it-yourselfers install them every week. As with hardwood flooring, careful planning and taking your time makes the difference with tile floors.

Buying

Where can you buy flooring material? Because many flooring products for the do-it-yourselfer are commodities, you can find them virtually anywhere. Hardware stores, building material retailers, flooring stores (obviously!), and even discount chains carry popular types and brands. And yes, you can also find flooring materials on the Internet. I recently purchased 800 square feet of prefinished solid hardwood flooring that way!

However, the best place to start looking typically is at a large flooring store. Why? Because it will have the greatest selection. In addition, you can get the best advice from the pros there. The store's prices may be higher than at a building materials supplier, but the advice and selection may be worth the difference. Ask about discounts, sales, and closeouts to bring the price even lower.

Wherever you buy, make sure you can get information and service after the sale—especially if this is your first flooring project.

Preparing the Subfloor

How much preparation the basement subfloor requires depends on its material and condition as well as what you're installing on it.

All concrete floors seem to draw moisture, passing it on to whatever is in contact, such as your new floor. So, at the least, you will need to install a vapor barrier below new flooring. Then comes the adhesive or wood depending on whether you're gluing or nailing the new flooring down.

Patching

There are numerous concrete repair products available through local building material suppliers. The best choice depends on the severity of the damage (crack, hole, slippage) and its size. In extreme cases, it may be best to remove a large section of concrete slab and replace it with a new one rather than make numerous patches. The goal is to provide a sufficiently smooth and level base for the new flooring material.

Construction Zone

Make sure you wear protective gear when working with concrete repair and leveling products. The fine dust can irritate your lungs and eyes. Wear a protective breathing mask and safety glasses.

Patch products are available for repairing concrete floor cracks.

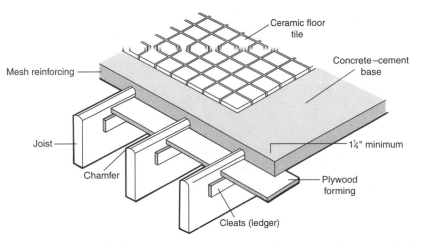

Ceramic floor tile

Concrete–cement base

Mesh reinforcing

Joist

Chamfer

1¼" minimum

Plywood forming

Cleats (ledger)

Components of a typical tile floor over wood using a backing panel, called a backerboard.

Leveling

Products are available that you mix and thickly spread on a concrete floor to smooth out any uneven areas. They can fill in as much as an inch in height. The pros at your flooring or building material store can tell you more and show you how they work.

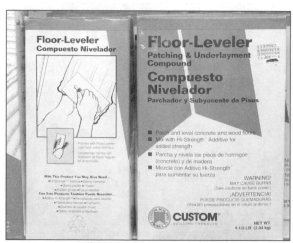

Leveling products are designed to level concrete up to 1 inch.

Leveling products are relatively easy to use, but messy.

Alternatively, you can install strips of wood over the concrete and attach a new plywood subfloor to it. The flooring then is attached to the new subfloor. (See Chapter 6 for instructions on installing a subfloor.)

Surfacing

Common underlayment materials for flooring include hardboard, particleboard, plywood, cement backerboard, and mastic with binders (latex, asphalt, polyvinyl-acetate). From the list you can see that underlayment is either rigid or thick viscous. In addition, floors with moisture problems need a moisture barrier, typically some type of plastic sheeting.

Backerboard is installed under ceramic tile floors.

Mastic is an adhesive with a thickener or binder. The thickener gives the mastic bulk so it can be troweled smooth and level. In addition, some flooring mastics can help waterproof the subfloor, keeping moisture away from the flooring materials. Other flooring mastics retain some elasticity and adhesion after installation, making them an excellent flooring adhesive as well.

Various flooring adhesives.

Installing Flooring

Once the subfloor is solid, level, and clean you can start installing your new basement flooring. Actual installation procedures depend on what you bought. Fortunately, most flooring products today come with at least some installation instructions. Even so, let's take a look at how it's done.

Basement flooring can be mixed depending on area use.

Painting the Floor

If a concrete floor is okay with you, or you just don't want to hassle with all of the other options, consider painting your concrete basement floor. It's a popular alternative.

The best products are epoxy paints made specifically for concrete basement and garage floors. They come in a wide range of colors. However they can be difficult to apply. If you select this product, read all the instructions and heed all the warnings because, once down, the finish won't come up easily.

The alternative is oil-based or latex paints. They are easier to apply, however they won't hold up as long. Fortunately, some of the newer products balance ease of installation with wearability to provide a good product that you can apply yourself. Try your favorite paint and building material stores to learn what's available.

Installing Floating Laminate Flooring

Laminate flooring is very popular with do-it-yourselfers because it is relatively easy to install. A floating floor is one that isn't directly attached to the subfloor below or to the walls. Each piece interlocks with its neighbor to form a continuous flooring surface. Laminate flooring that is installed in bathrooms, kitchens, and other potentially wet areas should be installed with a waterproof seam glue. Follow manufacturer's instructions for best results.

Make sure you first install a moisture barrier below the new floor, especially if it's above concrete, because ground moisture and condensation can damage most flooring materials.

Insert spacers between the wall and the first row to allow space for the floating floor to expand and contract with humidity.

Select the tools you'll need for installation. Here are a hammer, wall spacers, pull bar, and tapping block, components of a laminate flooring installation kit available through retailers.

Cut the last piece in the first row to fit, allowing ¼-inch space on the side wall for expansion.

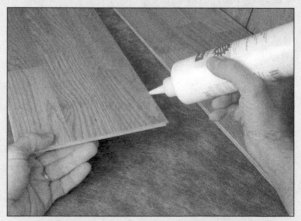

Use the flooring manufacturer's recommended adhesive for gluing the edges of the interlocking boards as you install the second and subsequent rows.

Interlock the laminate board edges together, making sure that excess glue is removed.

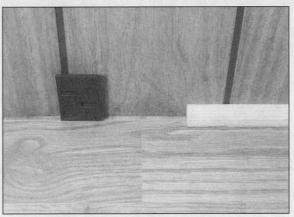

Use the tapping block to make sure that the laminate board interlocks with other boards in the same row.

Use the pull bar and a hammer to ensure that the boards fit snugly with no gap between them. Be careful to not damage the board edges.

Once the flooring is installed, remove the spacer and use trim to cover the gap between the floating floor and the wall.

Installing Wood Flooring

Hardwood flooring may be difficult to install in a moist basement or on top of concrete. However, if the basement is dry and you install a solid underlayment that can accept nails a hardwood floor is a beautiful addition. Hardwood is the wood of broadleaf trees, such as maple, oak, and birch. Although hardwood is usually harder than softwood, it isn't as hard as laminate or vinyl flooring materials.

Wood has been a popular flooring material for hundreds of years. In the past it was solid wood boards, then someone started milling them so that they fit together tightly—called *tongue-and-groove* milling. As solid wood became more expensive, laminate products increased in popularity. Laminate flooring has a melamine coating on top of either a thin ply of real wood or a *photo* of real wood, and underlying plies of high-density particle board.

Deeper Meaning

Tongue-and-groove is a method of milling lumber so that it fits together tightly and forms an extremely strong floor. Tongue-and-groove boards are milled with a tongue, or projecting rib, on one edge and a matching groove on the other.

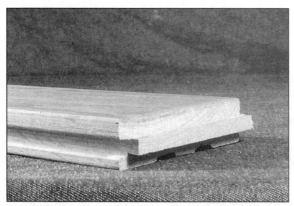

Typical tongue-and-groove flooring material.

Solid wood flooring typically is made up of ¾-inch thick tongue-and-groove hardwood. Strip flooring is under 3 inches wide and plank flooring is over 3 inches wide. Oak is the most popular hardwood flooring material though many people prefer cherry, walnut, or maple.

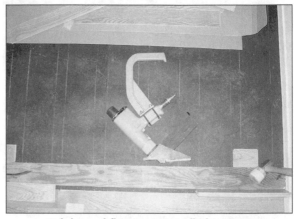

Solid wood flooring is installed in rows with a special flooring nailer.

Installation is relatively easy. Starting at the room's longest wall, the first row is laid against the wall and on top of the underlayment (builder's felt is preferred). The top edge closest to the wall is face-nailed and the tongue is angle-nailed. Then each subsequent row of boards is pressed against the prior row so that the groove fits over the tongue and nailed only at the tongue. Space the nails about 6 inches apart and no closer than 2 inches from board ends.

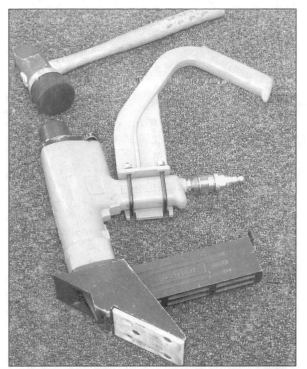

Hardwood flooring nailers can be rented
at floor shops or rental centers.

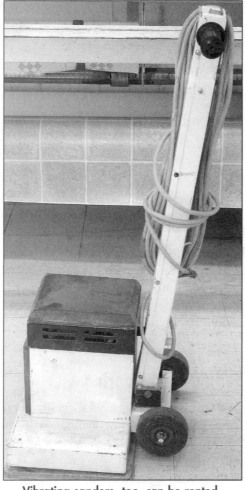

Vibrating sanders, too, can be rented.

If you're installing prefinished hardwood
flooring, the job is about done. However, if
you're installing unfinished hardwood, you still
need to sand the floor surface smooth and
apply a finish. You can rent a hardwood floor
sander from rental stores. The finish you select
can be a stain, a sealer, or a combination. Your
flooring supplier can make recommendations
based on use and traffic.

Prefinished solid wood flooring
is installed tongue to groove.

The finished floor is ready for traffic.

Vinyl flooring comes in sheets that can be cut, glued, and rolled.

Laminate flooring is relatively easy to install. Most interlock and float on the subfloor with no adhesion. Laminate flooring manufacturers include specific instructions with their product, typically packed in boxes of about 20 square feet.

Installing Vinyl Flooring

Vinyl flooring materials are especially popular with do-it-yourselfers who are finishing their basement. Vinyl is a good choice for areas where moisture is a potential problem. It comes in sheets and is easy to cut (though not always easy to handle and lay). It holds up well to heavy traffic. And it's relatively inexpensive.

Fortunately, you can buy vinyl flooring in either sheets or squares. Squares resolve the bulk issue of sheet vinyl but they introduce a new one: seepage. Water can seep between 12-inch-square vinyl tiles and damage the subfloor below. However, a good vapor barrier, waterproof adhesive, and careful installation can prevent a seepage problem and make vinyl squares just about the easiest flooring to install. You can purchase tiles and adhesive separately or self-adhesive tiles with glue already on the bottom (and covered with a removable paper). Some contractors prefer to install vinyl tile with mastic adhesive rather than self-adhesive tile.

The easiest vinyl tile to install is self-adhesive squares.

Some vinyl tile is made to look like wood.

Once the vinyl tile is installed, use a heavy roller to press it into the adhesive. Rollers can be rented.

Installing Tile Flooring

In some ways, tile is easier to install than hardwood flooring, especially over basement concrete. Tile requires a firm surface because movement in the tile caused by furniture and traffic can crack unsupported tile.

Ceramic and porcelain tile floors are beautiful additions to a basement.

Most folks opt for ceramic or porcelain tile in either 9-inch or 12-inch squares. You can mix and match colors—and even sizes—to come up with a unique pattern.

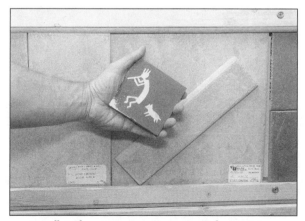

Smaller tile squares can serve as inlay or trim.

Inlay decorative tile for a unique design.

Tile installation requires spreading a mastic or adhesive into which the tiles are set. Temporary plastic spacers between the tiles keep them at the proper distance for the next step. Once the adhesive is cured, spread the floor with grout, working it into the space between tiles at an angle to ensure the space is packed tightly with grout. Select the mastic and grout based on the tile manufacturer's or retailer's recommendations.

The final step is adding the grout or colored adhesive between tiles.

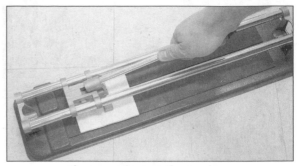

If you need to cut tile, purchase or borrow a small tile cutter.

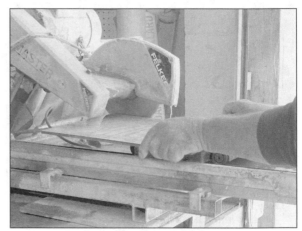

For large tile cutting jobs, borrow or rent a wet tile cutter.

Installing Carpeting

Carpet is not always the first choice for do-it-yourselfers. The primary reason is not the difficulty but the size. Carpeting comes in heavy rolls of 12-, 13.5-, and 15-feet widths. If you're young and strong, or have helpers who are, consider carpeting for your basement.

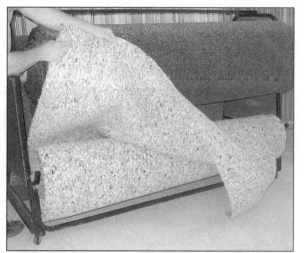

Carpet pad is purchased by the square foot or square yard in various densities.

The steps to installing carpet are to first install carpet tack strips around the perimeter of the room, then lay a carpet pad between the strips to cover the subfloor. If you're attaching tack strips to cement make sure you get ones made especially for this application. Some have masonry nails in them for fastening to the concrete while others rely on an adhesive.

The carpet pad is rolled out and cut at the wall's edge.

On the Level

Remodelers say "don't be afraid of installing your own carpeting." If you take your time and get good advice from your carpet retailer (and this book) you can install carpeting throughout a basement in just a few days.

The trick to carpeting is seaming it or attaching two pieces together. If you're working with smaller rooms this may not even be an issue. Cutting the edge is relatively easy using a carpet knife run around the room's perimeter at the base of the wall. Carpets require stretching, but you can rent the tools and get a demonstration at your carpet store or tool rental center. Once the carpet is fully stretched you can do a final trim and make sure that the edges are securely attached to the tack strips.

Seaming a carpet requires specialized tools.

Carpeting stairs takes more time, but can be done by the do-it-yourselfer.

Finishing Flooring

You're not done quite yet! Once the flooring is installed and the walls are painted (see Chapter 12) you can install trim around the floor's perimeter. *Trim* includes a baseboard at the bottom or base of the wall. Baseboard molding can be installed before or after carpeting is installed. If you've installed flooring materials that have a gap between the flooring and the wall (hardwood, laminate, tile, etc.) you'll want to cover the gap with quarter-round trim.

Deeper Meaning

Trim is any finish materials in a structure that are placed to provide decoration or to cover the joints between surfaces or contrasting materials. Door and windows casings, baseboards, picture moldings, and cornices are examples of trim.

Most trim is installed by nailing or stapling it in place. The baseboard is attached to the wall and nails go into the wall studs. Quarter-round trim is fastened to the baseboard. Alternatively, vinyl flooring often is trimmed with a vinyl splash molding, especially in rooms that may get a wet floor such as a kitchen or bathroom. The vinyl trim comes in rolls and is installed using an adhesive.

Finally, install thresholds or transitions between rooms of different flooring materials. Two adjacent rooms with vinyl tile don't require a threshold, but the seam where carpet and tile or another flooring material meets should be covered. In addition, install a riser threshold if one of the floors is lower than the other.

Thresholds can serve as transitions
between two types of flooring materials.

Various threshold products can be
purchased through building supply retailers.

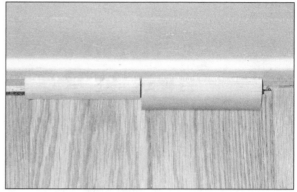

Make sure that the quarter-round trim
installed covers the gap at the wall.

The Least You Need to Know

◆ Basement flooring can be both decorative
and functional if planned well and
installed carefully.

◆ Make sure the basement's subfloor is
smooth and prepared for the flooring
material you plan to install.

◆ You have many flooring options no matter what your skill level and budget—and
new products make the job easier for the
do-it-yourselfer.

◆ The final step is to trim the flooring
where it meets the wall and where it
meets different flooring material used in
other rooms.

In This Part

Decorating Your Basement

Congratulations! You've planned and remodeled your unfinished basement without angering the neighbors or losing a limb. The basement is finished—almost. All you need to do is paint it, furnish it, and add some finishing touches.

Once the walls are up and electric lights work, many folks want to start moving in. Avoid the urge as long as you can because decorating will be much easier now. You have room to paint without painting the furniture. You can then start moving the larger furniture and appliances in, then add the decorating touches that make it your home. And that's what finishing your basement is all about.

Enjoy!

In This Chapter

- ◆ Choosing your basement colors
- ◆ What tools will you need?
- ◆ Preparing and painting walls and ceilings
- ◆ Painting doors, windows, and trim
- ◆ Wallpapering your basement

Chapter **12**

Painting or Wallpapering Your Basement

When is the best time to paint and decorate your basement? It depends on the design, how it is finished, and who is doing the work. You can add paint and wallpaper after drywall is up and either before or after the flooring is installed. If you're using paneling instead of drywall you may opt to paint the ceiling once it's in and the trim after doors, windows, and flooring are in. The *best* time is when new paint will not be damaged by other work.

In this chapter, I'll show you how to paint walls, ceilings, and trim. You'll learn how to pick colors, paint, and tools. In addition, I'll show you how to install wallpaper the easy way, adding design to your basement with little effort.

Selecting Paints and Tools

The first step in decorating your basement is choosing the type of wall covering you want: paint or wallpaper. Paint is by far the most popular because it's easy to apply by even inexperienced painters. And the newer paints make application nearly foolproof.

Selecting Paints

You know that sunlight seems to change the shade of paint colors on a wall or ceiling. Unfortunately, many basements don't have much natural light. Even artificial light impacts how colors are seen. Here are some tips for selecting paint colors based on natural and artificial light:

- Consider your flooring colors when selecting paint, even if the flooring isn't in yet. Also consider the colors of furniture and drapes that will be placed in the room.

- Apply cool colors (green, blue, violet, gray) on walls that receive warm natural light such as from the south or west.

- Select warm colors (red, orange, brown, yellow) for walls that get cool natural light from the north and east.

- Buy samples of selected colors and apply them to a section of a wall to see how they look in the room with installed lighting.

- Smaller rooms seem larger if all surfaces are of the same or lighter colors.

- Accent a room by painting one wall a color compatible with that on the other walls.

- Deemphasize a long room by painting the walls on opposite ends with a darker color or shade.

- Select colors based on the use and desired mood of the room; your paint store can help.

Paint stores and large hardware stores have a variety of tools for selecting and installing paints.

What colors should you consider for your new basement rooms? The answer depends on what mood you want for the room. Here are some decorator tips:

- Blues and turquoises are refreshing and tranquil.

- Earth tones are warm and cozy.

- Gold and bronze are rich and friendly.

- Gray-greens, aquas, and jades are calm and serene.

- Grays, charcoals, and neutrals are cool and receding.

- Greens are cheerful and open.

- Olive tones are somber and quiet.

- Oranges and peaches are active and inviting.

- Pinks and reds are lively and aggressive.

- Purples and violet blues are sophisticated and daring.

- Yellows and lime are bright and sunny.

Dark wall paint can reduce the perceived light in a basement room.

White and light paints enhance lighting.

Make sure that hallways have brighter
paints and sufficient lighting.

Besides colors, consider the properties you want your painted walls to have. Oil-based (alkyd resin) paints seem richer, but are moderately more difficult to apply and clean up. Latex paints are easier to apply and clean, and are available in various glosses.

Of course, the paint you select depends on what it's going to cover. Masonry paint has properties very different from paint used to cover drywall or wood. Application is slightly different, too. Fortunately, paint containers offer information on what the paint covers and how to apply it.

This dark color is contrasted by light
ceiling and floor colors.

Light colors can brighten a stairway
and make it more safe.

How much paint will you need? Depending on whether you're first applying a primer coat and how porous the surface is, most paints suggest that a gallon can cover about 400 square feet. That's approximately four walls in a 10 by-15-feet room. Actual coverage can range from about 300 to 500 square feet per gallon. The paint container will offer guidelines and an experienced paint store clerk can give you advice.

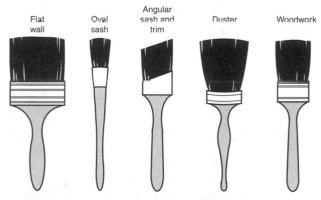

Various popular painting brushes.

Construction Zone

Remember to recycle paint cans by cleaning them out, allowing them to dry, then removing the residue in the can. Latex paint cans typically can be recycled with other cans. Oil-based paint cans may require recycling as hazardous waste. If you're not sure, ask your local paint retailer.

Selecting Tools

You don't *need* many tools to paint a basement. A brush is about all that's necessary. However, you can make the job easier with a few other inexpensive tools:

- A paint roller and tray lets you put more paint on the wall faster.
- A roll of plastic drop cloth can make cleanup easier.
- Masking tape makes it easier to paint up to the edge of another surface.
- An edge roller minimizes masking and cuts job time.
- An airless paint sprayer can dramatically cut application time, although it adds to the prep and cleanup.

Your paint or hardware store will have a variety of brushes and related tools.

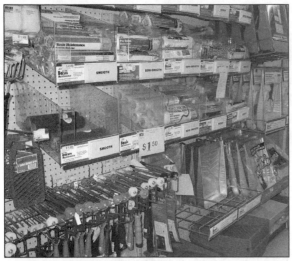

Paint rollers come in all sizes, grades, and applications.

On the Level

If you're doing much painting, invest in a lamb's-wool roller, typically less than $15. Not only will it hold more paint and apply it more smoothly, it's also easier to clean up than other rollers.

Preparing Surfaces for Paint

Once you've selected the paint and tools you need, the next job is to prepare the surfaces for paint. Fortunately, many of the surfaces are new and relatively clean. However, masonry foundation walls will need a thorough cleaning and preparation to accept new paint.

Even new basement surfaces will have dust and splatters from the work that's been going on. Use TSP (trisodium phosphate) or another cleaner recommended by your paint supplier to thoroughly clean the surface. Note that most cleaners will need a final rinse with clean water. Remember to wear protective gloves when working with cleaners.

If any patching is required to masonry, drywall, or other surfaces, now is the time to take care of it. Follow the directions on the masonry patch container, removing loose debris and applying the patch in layers until you have a smooth, dry surface. You can patch drywall with one of the popular patch kits and a container of wet patch.

Some paint manufacturers suggest a primer coat before the paint is applied. A primer seals the surface and gives the paint a good surface on which to bond. In addition, primer can help transition from the wall color to the chosen paint color. A good primer can minimize the number of paint coats required, thus saving time.

Painting a room typically means painting only specific surfaces—not window glass, door trim, flooring, and other surfaces. The best way to not get paint on an adjacent surface is to mask it, or use masking tape to cover the first inch or two of the surface that doesn't need painting. Two-inch masking tape is most popular. If necessary, attach the tape to the edge of a plastic drop cloth to keep paint off larger surfaces such as flooring.

On the Level

Don't buy cheap masking tape; it can be difficult to remove and leave a residue. Instead, pay a dollar or two more for the better stuff and save yourself some grief!

Painting Your Basement

It's time to start painting. Here are some tips for painting walls, ceilings, doors, windows, and trim:

◆ Make sure the room you're painting has adequate ventilation.

◆ If you are sensitive to chemicals, wear a painter's mask and gloves.

◆ Paint the ceiling before painting the walls.

◆ Use a trim or chisel brush to "cut in" or paint areas next to moldings and in corners where the roller can't easily get.

◆ Paint from top to bottom with smooth strokes.

◆ Once you start painting a wall don't stop until the wall is done so the paint dries evenly.

◆ Use a brush or roller extension when painting a ceiling, or use a *safe* platform that brings you nearer the surface.

◆ Airless sprayers can make the job go much faster, however they require more skill; practice on an easier job before using it to paint your basement.

◆ Use a paint shield, a flat metal or plastic piece with a handle, to shield adjacent surfaces from paint spatter.

◆ Dip the paint brush no more than halfway into the paint; let the bristles soak up paint, and then wipe the excess from the tip.

◆ Wipe excess paint from the roller before lifting it from the pan to minimize dripping and spatter.

◆ Roll paint on the wall in an M pattern about 3 feet square, then add crosswise strokes to fill the pattern.

◆ If necessary, apply a second coat of paint once the first coat is dry.

Having said all that, I'll tell you next about painting specific surfaces. Take a break.

Painting Drywall

Most interior basement walls will be made of drywall (see Chapter 10). One reason drywall is so popular is because of its paintability. The paper cover is smooth and readily absorbs paint. It frequently doesn't require a primer coat, saving time and expense.

The downside of drywall is that the paint dries quickly. It's also an advantage, but it means that you can't stop in the middle of a wall for lunch. You should finish painting to a corner or, if possible, the entire room including trim. Otherwise, you may be able to see where you took a break. However, glossy paints tend to show touch-ups more readily than flat paints.

Painting Wood

Depending on your basement design you can paint the wood trim, doors, and windows the same color as the room or an accent color. In addition, you can decide to apply a wood stain, a paintlike product that has less pigment or color in it, allowing the wood's grain to show through. Some trim woods have little grain and should be painted, but oak or other wood with character look best when stained.

Painting Masonry

Painting masonry, concrete, or concrete blocks is similar to painting any other flat surface. However, because masonry is porous, it typically requires a primer coat so the paint will adhere. Good-quality masonry primer also can cover up any water stains. In addition, some masonry primers seal the surface against moisture.

If painting masonry, select rollers specifically designed for the job. They can help work the primer or paint into the surface.

Cleaning Up

Cleaning up latex paint is relatively easy because it's water-soluble. You can soak hardened brushes until they are soft, then rinse them thoroughly to remove excess paint. Remember that brushes and rollers are designed to absorb lots of paint so rinsing all of the paint out may take awhile. Run water over and through tools until the water runs clear.

Cleaning up after applying an oil-based paint is a little more work. It requires a paint solvent. Wear protective gloves and follow directions on the container.

Wallpapering

For instant decoration, apply wallpaper to basement walls alongside or instead of paint. Wallpapering used to be a difficult job that required finesse and a few @#&*% words. Today's wall covering products are much easier to apply, especially the ones with adhesive already on the back side.

Preparing Walls

Preparing for wallpaper means making sure the wall surface is clean, dry, and smooth. Use TSP (trisodium phosphate) or other cleaner to clean dirty surfaces. Otherwise, use a vacuum cleaner and a brush to remove any dust particles left over from remodeling your basement.

Installing Wallpaper

The most difficult part of installing wallpaper is aligning it so that seams and any vertical patterns match up. You don't want to be able to see the seams.

Wallpaper installation tools.

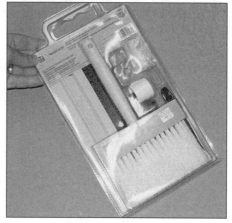

Wallpaper installation kit.

The wall covering product you purchase will have installation instructions. However, most are installed in the same manner. The first sheet is installed vertically next to an inconspicuous corner such as behind the room's door. Mark the wall with a vertical starting line and align the paper's edge to it. Then continue around the room, aligning and overlapping each sheet to match the pattern. Carefully cut out around windows, doors, and electrical fixtures.

Adding Trim

Trim is multifunctional. It not only offers a decorative accent, it covers the rough edges of construction. For example, you made a rectangular hole in the wall then inserted a prehung door in the rough opening. There's a gap between the wall and door frames. That's where trim can help.

Because finishing your basement is more like new construction than remodeling you can do what builders do: Paint (or wallpaper) and *then* trim. That saves you the task of masking off door, window, and floor trim as you paint walls. In many homes, trim is installed in two stages, depending on what flooring is installed and when the walls are painted.

Modern trim is relatively easy to install. That's because trim pieces come in standard designs and lengths to make construction easier. In many cases, all that's needed is to cut the trim to length and fasten it in place.

Trim is cut either perpendicular (90 degrees) or diagonal (45 degrees) to the long edge. The favorite tool for this is the miter box, a fine-toothed saw and a three-sided box with slits that align the saw for 45-degree, 90-degree, and other popular degree cuts.

Fasten trim with finish nails (the ones with a small head), use a nail set to indent them below the wood surface, then fill in the hole with wood filler and paint.

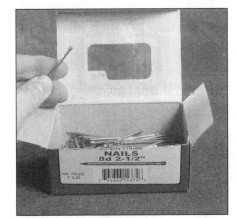

Finish nails.

On the Level

When nailing finish nails into wood, stop before the head is near the surface (so you don't strike the wood) and use a nail set or punch to drive the nail head below the wood surface. Finally, fill the hole in with wood putty of the same color as the trim.

The Least You Need to Know

◆ Masonry basement walls require special paint to adhere to the concrete without chipping or cracking.

◆ For best results, prepare the drywall, wood, or masonry surface by cleaning and smoothing it to absorb the paint well.

◆ Using quality painting tools can make the job easier and the paint last longer.

◆ Taking your time while painting means less excess paint to clean up off other surfaces.

◆ Wallpaper and other wall coverings are a popular—and easy—alternative to paint.

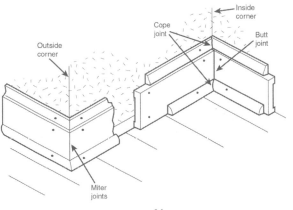

Various types of base trim.

In This Chapter

- ◆ Installing cabinets and countertops
- ◆ Moving furniture into the basement
- ◆ Adding entertainment systems
- ◆ Setting up a home office in your basement

Chapter

Furnishing Your Basement

Wow! Your unfinished basement is looking almost finished. You're not ready to move in yet—unless you'll sit and sleep on the floor! But you're nearly done.

This chapter gets you to moving-in day. It includes adding cabinets and countertops for kitchens, bathrooms, and other rooms. It also helps you furnish what may become the most popular rooms in your new basement: the home office and the entertainment room.

Eager to get started? I'll bet! Let's get this job *done*.

Installing Cabinets in Your Basement

Chances are that your new basement needs some cabinets. They may be for a bathroom or kitchenette, or you're installing built-in bookshelves or counters in a new office or entertainment center. And chances are that these are already included in your remodeling plan. You know their size and location. But maybe you haven't selected the exact cabinet yet.

Typical cabinet installation.

If you've planned plumbing without cabinets, install the final fixtures.

You can build cabinets into basement closets for more storage.

Selecting Cabinets

Custom cabinets can be beautiful. They're also expensive. If your budget allows, consider at least one custom cabinet for your new basement. Maybe it's for the entertainment center or a wet bar, somewhere with high visibility. Otherwise, you'll find that stock cabinets are quite adequate, and the better ones are solid and decorative. Don't pass them by without considering them.

Cabinets are available in standardized sizes. That makes the selection and installation job easier. In addition, local building codes tell you how high to install hanging cabinets, so the guesswork is reduced. However, there still are decisions to make when selecting cabinets, such as style and quality.

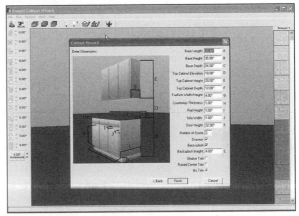

Design software can help you design your basement cabinets.

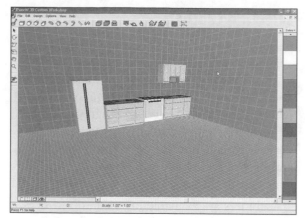
Software also can help you place cabinets.

Cabinet trim materials are available at building suppliers.

The two types of cabinets are framed and frameless. Framed cabinets are the traditional style that use oak and other decorative woods with exposed hinges. Frameless cabinets are more contemporary with flat surfaces, often covered in a colored melamine and with concealed hinges. There are hybrid cabinets as well with some of the features of each.

You can purchase and stain panels for cabinet sides.

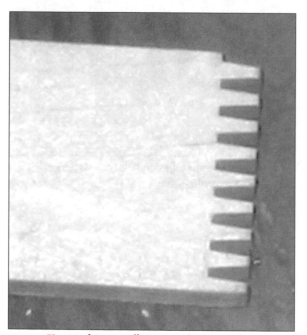
Finer cabinets will use interlocking joints.

Setting Cabinets

Base cabinets are relatively easy to place. Here's how it's done:

1. Mark a *level* reference line on the wall where cabinets will be installed so that the tops of all base cabinets will be level.

2. Cut any holes necessary in the back of the cabinet for plumbing or wiring.

3. Place the cabinet (the corner cabinet if more than one) and use shims to level the top at the reference line.

4. Move shims as needed to make sure that the cabinet is plumb and level.

5. Install any adjacent cabinets.

6. Use screws to fasten the cabinet into wall studs; use a stud finder to identify locations if not known.

7. Install toe-kick molding to cover the bottom front edge of the cabinet and trim molding where cabinets meet.

Your base cabinets are now ready for countertops.

Hanging or wall cabinets are installed in a similar way. Mark the wall for level, place the cabinet, then attach it to the wall with screws into the studs.

Built-in cabinets are trimmed to the wall and ceiling.

Large freestanding entertainment center.

Base and wall cabinets.

Large built-in cabinet.

**There are many countertop tiles
from which to choose.**

Installing Countertops

Countertops for single cabinets are relatively easy to install. You can buy them to fit standard cabinets and fasten them from below. Make sure that the screws you use aren't so long that they will pop up through the countertop.

If you have a group of cabinets such as in a kitchen or as built-ins in a den or office, you may need to build your own countertops in place—or have them built for you. That's because there's a wide variety of cabinet group designs and there aren't that many standard groupings.

Fortunately, planning and installing countertops isn't that difficult. Many do-it-yourselfers opt to install ceramic tile over a sturdy plywood counter base. Installation is similar to that of installing tile floors (see Chapter 11), on a smaller scale. Alternatively, you can install a plastic laminate, sometimes known by the Formica brand name, on the plywood counter base. The top is installed with a special (and caustic) adhesive, rolled smooth, and trimmed with a power router. Then the facing edge is installed in the same manner. Check your building material supplier for more options and more specific directions.

Installed countertop.

Your cabinet is now ready for installing plumbing fixtures (as explained in Chapter 7).

Construction Zone _____

Be very careful working around countertop adhesives. Prolonged exposure may cause respiratory problems. Make sure you read and heed the directions on the container.

Finally, install plumbing fixtures.

Placing Furniture

Ready to sit down or take a nap in your new basement? Not quite yet! You need furniture first.

You probably already have an idea of how you're going to place the furniture in your new basement. Or you're waiting to see the finished product before you decide. In either case, think *access*. That is, how will you get the furniture in and out of the basement? That's why you'll appreciate local building code that requires doorways and stairs to be of a specific size. You need to get that extra couch into the basement without marring all the walls.

If you have large furniture that may be difficult to move to the basement, consider bringing it in during the remodeling process and building around it. Alternatively, hold off adding stair rails or other trim that will reduce the entryway size until the larger pieces are in.

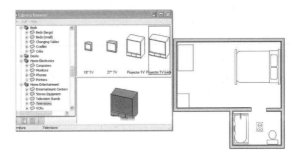
Remodeling software can make virtual furniture easier on your back.

Furniture turns a room into a living space.

Start moving larger furniture in first.

Then move in decorative pieces such as rugs and lamps.

Everything's moved in and ready for occupancy.

When placing furniture in a room, start with the largest pieces in the farthest room from the stairs. Then add the smaller things in that same room. That will keep you from tripping over things as you bring additional furniture in. Of course, if you have a daylight or walkout basement with an entry door, the job will be much easier than carrying things through the house and down the basement stairs.

Find a new rug that fits your finished basement.

Installing Entertainment Systems

Our parents probably never considered dedicating an entire room to "entertainment." However, they didn't have cable, satellite, DVDs, CDs, and SurroundSound. Nor did they have digital video cameras. Today's families often have many and some have all of these entertainment toys—and more!

So what do you do with it all? The latest trend is to put it all in a single room, the entertainment room or home theater. And it's a popular reason why people are finishing their basements.

This topic was introduced in Chapter 3 on designing your basement. At that time you may have included such systems in your remodeling plan. In fact, you also installed required wiring (see Chapter 8). If so, let's connect everything up.

On the Level

If one or more basement rooms won't be in use yet, use them for temporary storage or as a staging area. If you have a crew, the drones can take things to the staging room and the queen (or king) bees can move things to the appropriate rooms.

Installing Cable or Satellite

If your basement is prewired for cable or satellite you have an entrance box that feeds the system. The signal to the box comes either from your local cable provider or from a subscription satellite dish mounted on or near your home. Following your building plan, wiring was installed to terminal boxes in various rooms. It's now show time!

Fortunately, connecting these systems is relatively easy once the wiring is run. You can purchase wall plates at Radio Shack or other electronic suppliers. To wire the back side of the wall plate, follow directions that come with it. Once the plate's installed, the appropriate entertainment device can be plugged in or screwed on to the plate face.

Make sure you purchase the correct plate and connector for entertainment and computer systems. Television systems use F connectors, telephones use RJ11 connectors, coax cable connectors are labeled RG58, and computer networks use RG45 or Cat 5 connectors.

Installing Sound Systems

Stereo systems can be heard throughout your new basement if you've prewired it for sound—or if you turn the volume *way* up.

Connecting up the system typically means installing wall plates that include terminals for left and right channels. The wall plate can have a local volume control on it and even be wired for an intercom. As with other systems, these need to be planned in advance of remodeling so that wiring goes to the appropriate locations.

The final step is simply installing the wall plate or sound controller/intercom to the wiring.

Installing Business Furniture

Did you plan and build a home office in your new basement? If so, it's time to furnish it with all the tools (and toys) needed to put it to work.

Placing Office Furniture

What will you be doing in your new home office/den? Paying bills? Taking work home from the office? Building a new business? Will the kids do their homework in it? How you will use the room—and your budget—will dictate what office furniture you need and can afford for your new home office.

At least you'll need a desk. It can be a student desk for less than $100 or an office suite with pedestal desk, credenza, and bridge for $2,000 or more. Whatever fits your needs—and whatever money you have left over from remodeling. Just make sure that you don't buy any new office or other furniture for your basement unless you're *sure* you can get it down there.

Borrowing Furniture from Other Rooms

Before shopping for new furniture for your home office, look around the other areas of your home. It may be that you can pull some excess furniture and accessories from crowded rooms on the upper floors to furnish your office or den. It can become the new location for all those boxed books in the garage, that extra bookcase in your bedroom, or that desk no one's using in the living room. You have loads of options now that you have more living space!

Installing Computers and Networks

Computers don't require anything special other than an electrical outlet for the CPU and monitor. However, if you'll be spending some time online you'll need a telephone outlet for the modem. And if you have more than one computer in your home (ours currently has four with a fifth on the way) you can connect them into a network.

Wireless computer networks may not be in your remodeling budget. That means you need to make sure your office and any other associated rooms have network access. Once the wires are in the walls, connecting them up is relatively easy using wall plates available through your computer supplier or an electronics store. Directions come with them.

I'll talk more about wireless systems in the next chapter.

Installing Phone Systems

Modems aren't the only use for telephone lines. People actually use them to talk on as well, and to send faxes. So hopefully your new basement plan has lots of telephone outlets, at least one in each new room.

Connecting up phone lines is relatively easy once the wiring is in place. Simply buy telephone wall plates and wire them following directions that come with the plate. Alternatively, you can remove an existing plate and see how it is wired. They are color coordinated: yellow to yellow, red to red, etc.

I'll cover telephone systems in greater detail in the next chapter.

The Least You Need to Know

- Make sure that the cabinets you install are level and plumb.
- Countertops for standard cabinets are easy to install; cabinet groups, however, may require the top be built in place.
- Move furniture into the farthest rooms from the stairs or daylight doorway first so they aren't in your way.
- Installing prewired cable, satellite, sound, telephone, and computer network systems is easy with special wall plates.

In This Chapter

- ◆ Adding a security system to your basement
- ◆ Installing or upgrading your communication systems
- ◆ Tips for decorating your basement
- ◆ Time to enjoy your new basement!

Chapter 14

Final Touches

Ready to move in? You've spent a lot of time and money finishing your basement, but it all pays off once you begin enjoying your new space. You can now separate the kids, give teens their own rooms, store foods, move grandma into her new apartment, start enjoying your new hobby room, watch movies or listen to music in your new home theater, or get to work in your home office.

Now it's time to add the final touches. For some basements, that means installing a security system or extending the phone or intercom system. For others, it's decorating the rooms. For everyone, it's celebrating your new space!

Installing Security Systems

The location of a basement often ensures security. A below-grade basement, for example, may allow entrance only through the house. Put some locks or sensors on any basement windows, install smoke detectors, and you're done. Daylight or walkout basements, however, may need additional security depending on where the entrance is. If access is from the street or an alley it may not be seen from the home's primary entrance and thus require more security measures.

On the Level _____

> If you're planning to add a security system to your home, consider hiring a security service or advisor to help you design it for optimum value. Also, it's less expensive to have a security system wire your home if the company can do so while the basement walls are open.

If you already have a security system in your home, chances are you need to at least extend it to your basement. If a security system contractor installed the primary system, let the contractor extend the system to your basement. If you installed it yourself, an extension may be relatively easy to put in.

Selecting Components

Security systems can include switches, sensors, auditory monitors, and controllers, and most systems have at least two of these components.

Switch circuits are either open or closed. A switch on a closed window or door is closed; if the window or door is opened the switch is open. The controller continuously checks to see if each switch is open or closed and, if open, sets off the alarm.

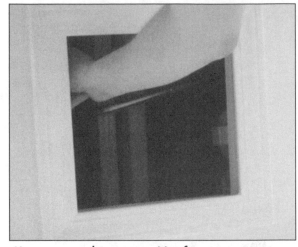

Use an access door to run wiring for your new systems.

Wiring can be hidden inside basement storage compartments.

There are various types of sensors, but they all work similar to a switch. They are either okay or not okay. For example, a smoke detector is okay until it senses smoke, then it's not okay and sets off an alarm. A motion sensor is okay if nothing moves in its sensory area; movement triggers the alarm. Vibration sensors work the same way, attached to window glass.

Make sure you install smoke detectors in your finished basement—especially if you have a fireplace.

The control panel is the brain of the operation. All switches and sensors report to it frequently. The control panel decides what to do with any open or not-okay reports. Actually, it only follows the orders of whoever set it up: *If open, call 9-1-1*, or *if not okay, sound alarm.*

Installation Steps

Basic security systems can be installed by the do-it-yourselfer. Components and kits can be purchased at retail electronic stores and larger hardware stores. The control panel module typically includes instructions for planning and installing it and the various components around the basement.

If you're adding to an existing security system, refer to the owner's manual for instructions. If that's not available, contact the manufacturer of the system. If all else fails, call a local security system installer for help or advice.

Fortunately, security systems are relatively easy to install. The control panel is centrally located and connected to power, then the various switches and sensors are installed at access points, typically doors and windows.

Smoke detectors are installed as connected or independent components of your security system. If the detector relies on house wiring for power, make sure it has some type of battery backup so it will work even if the lights go out.

Security switches and sensors are low-voltage devices. That means the wires running to them are relatively small and easier to hide. If you already installed the wiring (see Chapter 8) you need only attach and test the devices. If not, you need to also run the wiring between the device and the control panel. Otherwise, opt for wireless devices.

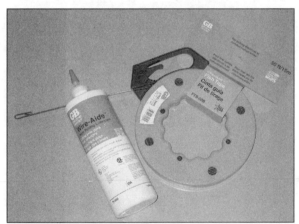

Forgot to prewire for security or phone? Use a fish tape to run new wiring (directions supplied).

Installing Communication Systems

Because the basement of your home is on a separate floor, communication is more difficult. "Hey, dad. The phone's for you!" "Can you bring me a peanut butter sandwich, hon?" "Gosh, the kids sure are *quiet* down there!" Fortunately, communication systems are relatively easy to install or upgrade—especially if you've planned for them. Let's take a look at how.

Installing Telephone Systems

Your basement remodeling plans probably included wiring for additional telephone jacks in basement rooms (see Chapter 8). You may even have called the phone company to install an extra line or two for your basement office, apartment, or teen room. So the finishing touch is to install telephone jacks in the various rooms.

Clearly mark prewired boxes
so installation is easier.

There are two types of phone jacks: flush and surface. A flush jack is one that is flush with the wall; there's a small box behind it into which the wires run. A surface jack is installed on the wall or baseboard and the wires are run either through the wall or behind the baseboard. Surface jacks are popular when extending a phone line without tearing up a wall for the wiring.

On the Level

Most residential telephone systems use a four-wire system: black, red, green, and yellow. Flush jacks and surface jacks, purchased at hardware and electronic stores, will have correspondingly colored terminals and wires inside of them. To install the jack, strip (remove the insulation) around the last ½-inch of each wire and attach it to the same-colored terminal.

Installing Intercom and Other Systems

If you've planned an intercom system you probably wired it up in Chapter 8. The finishing touch is to actually install the intercom boxes in the appropriate rooms. Fortunately, that's a relatively easy job because the system probably came with instructions.

In addition, many intercom systems can be attached to a stereo system so you can pipe music in to the various rooms. Don't expect high fidelity from most systems as they are set up to transfer voices, not music. (Imagine quality music through a drive-up window speaker!) If you want quality sound, prewire your basement for your sound system.

Satellite and audio systems are installed similarly. Wires must be run from the base unit to secondary equipment such as an entertainment center or speakers.

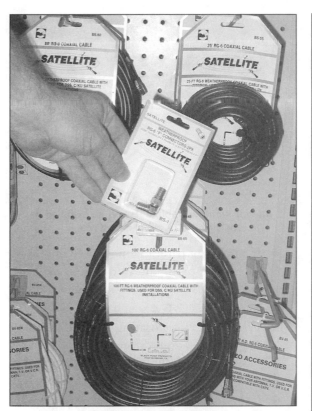

Satellite and cable wiring.

Installing Wireless Systems

Forgot to prewire for phones, intercom, or stereo system? No problem. You can probably "go wireless." In fact, you can even add a wireless network system so computers can talk with each other or send something to a printer.

Wireless systems require a transmitter and a receiver. Cordless phones, for example, have a base unit that transmits the voice and a hand unit that receives it. This type of system is also available for intercoms, stereos, security systems, and computers.

One of the problems with wireless intercoms, stereos, and such is the same problem that wireless phones face: interference. Some appliances, commercial radio transmitters, and other electronic devices can interfere with the signal. You probably don't want audible hum over your wireless stereo. One solution to this problem is to try before you buy. Use the device at your home for a few days to make sure there is no interference. Alternatively, electronic filters are available that can block out unwanted signals—for a price.

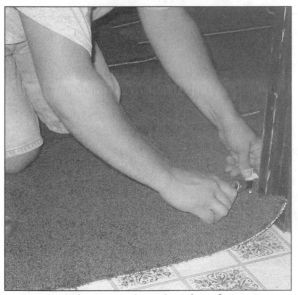

You can hide wiring along the edge of carpeting.

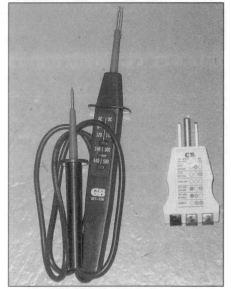

An electrical tester can help you verify that a circuit is off before working on it.

Decorating Your Basement

Final touches to your basement also means making it look lived in. No, that doesn't mean spreading dirty clothes over a teen's bedroom floor. It means adding favorite decorations in various rooms so residents feel "at home." Here are some ideas:

◆ Move some of the knickknacks and decorations from the main part of your house to the basement to make it feel more like home.

◆ If a child is moving to his or her new basement bedroom, ask what paint colors are preferred and let the child help do some of the painting and decorating (see Chapter 12 for painting tips).

Decorating can make your finished basement more enjoyable.

Interior window treatments can be installed to decorate a new basement room.

◆ If an elderly parent is moving in to a basement apartment, find and place decorative keepsakes in the room to make the transition easier.

◆ When you're decorating your home for the holidays, don't forget the basement. How about adding a small Christmas tree or other decorative touches?

◆ If the basement houses a getaway room for teens, get them involved in helping choose the decor.

◆ Make sure there is adequate lighting, especially in darker basement rooms, by adding lamps and other illuminations.

◆ If there is an outside entrance, make it secure and attractive.

◆ Add real and artificial plants (depending on available light) throughout living spaces.

An artificial plant can dress up a basement kitchen cabinet.

- If you've installed a new laundry room, make sure *everyone* feels comfortable using it—not just mom.
- If you've set up a home theater, add movie posters and memorabilia to enhance the ambiance. A candy counter would be nice, too!
- If you don't have room for a TV in your finished basement, consider hanging a small set from a wall.

Small wall TV.

Artificial plants also make good hall decorations.

- ◆ If one room is for music, put up decorations that set the mood for enjoyable practice and creative jams.
- ◆ Finish the stairway to your new basement with fastened carpeting and hand rails for safety.

Carpeting a basement stairway.

Hardware can be installed to hold the stair carpet in place.

Make sure the stair railing is installed for safety.

Decorating in Stages

Finished rooms are decorated in three stages. The first stage is the larger components depending on the room's function (bed, sofa, dining table). The second stage is supporting components (tables, rugs, chairs) that support the first stage. The final stage is adding items that complement the first two stages by function or design (lamps, pictures). Think of decorating a room from *big* to *small*.

An attractive entry to your new finished basement.

Need more decorating help? Check out the many books and magazines available on decorating, or tune in to one of the several TV shows that give decorating tips.

Enjoying Your Basement

Congratulations! You've finished your unfinished basement! Lots of work and money behind you—and lots of fun ahead.

So plan a basement party. Make it a below-grade open house. Invite neighbors, relatives, and friends over to share in enjoying your efforts. Now they will know why you've been making noise at odd hours and missed other people's parties. You've been finishing your basement!

Construction Zone

Don't forget that the higher value of your finished basement will increase your home's appraisal value—and your tax bill. Increase your household budget accordingly. Also, remember to update your homeowner's insurance policy for the value of your new finished basement and its contents.

Ah! Time to enjoy your new basement sauna.

The Least You Need to Know

◆ Finishing touches include installing a security system for your new finished basement.

◆ Finish installing the telephone, intercom, and wireless systems in your basement.

◆ Make your basement an integral part of your home by decorating it to your taste.

◆ Have a party to celebrate finishing your basement!

Basement Remodeling Glossary

ABS (acrylonitrile-butadine-styrene) Material used for rigid black plastic pipe in DWV systems.

air-dried lumber Lumber that has been dried naturally by air with a minimum moisture content of 15 to 20 percent.

apron The flat piece of inside trim that is placed against the wall directly under the sill of a window.

areaway An open subsurface space adjacent to a building used to admit light or air or as a means of access to a basement.

armored cable A flexible metal-sheathed cable used for indoor wiring. Commonly called BX cable.

backfill To push excavated earth into a trench around and against a basement foundation.

backhoe A machine that digs deep, narrow trenches for foundations and drains.

baluster A vertical member of the railing of a stairway, deck, balcony, or porch.

band joist A joist nailed across the ends of the floor or ceiling joists. Also called a *rim joist*.

baseboard A trim board placed at the base of the wall, next to the floor.

Baseboard.

Selection of prefinished baseboards.

basement The bottom story of a building below the first or ground floor. A basement may be partially or completely below surrounding grade.

base molding A strip of wood used to trim the upper edge of a baseboard.

beam A structural member, usually steel or heavy timber, used to support floor or ceiling joists or rafters.

bearing wall A wall that supports any vertical load in addition to its own weight.

blind-nailing Nailing in such a way that the nail heads are not visible on the face of the work.

blue lines or **blueprints** Reproductions of original construction documents that produce blue lines on a white background.

board foot A unit of lumber equal to a piece 1 foot square and 1 inch thick; 144 cubic inches of wood.

board lumber Yard lumber less than 2 inches thick and 2 or more inches wide.

bottom plate *See* soleplate.

box A metal or plastic container for electrical connections. More correctly called a *junction box*.

brace A piece of lumber or metal attached to the framing of a structure diagonally at an angle less than 90 degrees, providing stiffness or support.

branch In a plumbing or heating system, any part of the supply pipes connected to a fixture.

bridging Narrow wood or metal members placed on the diagonal between joists. Braces the joists and spreads the weight load.

builder's paper Usually, asphalt-impregnated paper of felt used in wall and roof construction; prevents the passage of air and moisture. Also known as building paper.

Builder's paper (15 pound and 30 pound).

building code   The collection of legal requirements for the construction of buildings.

building drain   The lowest horizontal drainpipe in a structure. Carries all waste out to the sewer.

cable   An electricity conductor made up of two or more wires contained in an overall covering.

cap plate   The framing member nailed to the top plates of stud walls to connect and align them. The uppermost of the two top plates, sometimes called the double-top plate.

carriage   In a stairway, the supporting member to which the treads and risers are fastened. Also called a *stringer*.

casement   A window sash on hinges attached to the sides of a window frame. Such windows are called casement windows.

casing   Moldings of various widths and forms; used to trim door and window openings between the jambs and the walls.

caulk   Viscous material used to seal joints and make them water- and airtight.

caulk gun   A tool used to apply caulk.

cellar   A room or group of rooms below or predominantly below grade, usually under a building.

check valve   A valve that lets water flow in only one direction in a pipe system.

circuit   The path of electric current as it travels from the source to the appliance or fixture and back to the source.

circuit breaker   A safety device used to interrupt the flow of power when the electricity exceeds a predetermined amount. Unlike a fuse, you can reset a circuit breaker.

Circuit breaker.

cleanout   An easy-to-reach and easy-to-open place in a DWV (drain-waste-vent) system where obstructions can be removed or a snake inserted.

Cleanout.

column   A vertical support—square, rectangular, or cylindrical—for a part of the structure above it.

common rafter   One of the parallel rafters, all the same length, that connect the eaves to the ridge board.

concrete A mixture of aggregates and cement that hardens to a stonelike form and is used for foundations, paving, and many other construction purposes.

conductor Any low-resistance material, such as copper wire, through which electricity flows easily.

conduit A metal, fiber, or plastic pipe or tube used to enclose electric wires or cables.

conventional mortgage An agreement between a buyer and a seller with no outside backing such as government insurance or guarantee.

countersinking Sinking or setting a nail or screw so that the head is flush with or below the surface.

cove molding A molding with a concave face. Usually used to trim or finish interior corners.

CPVC (chlorinated polyvinyl chloride) The rigid white or pastel-colored plastic pipe used for supply lines.

crawlspace A shallow space between the floor joists and the ground; usually enclosed by the foundation wall.

Crawlspace.

cripple studs Short studs surrounding a window or between the top plate and end rafter, in a gable end or between the foundation and subfloor. Also called *jack studs*.

cross-bridging Diagonal bracing between adjacent floor joists, placed near the center of the joist span to prevent joists from twisting.

crown molding A convex molding used horizontally wherever an interior angle is to be covered (usually at the top of a wall, next to the ceiling).

current The movement or flow of electrons, which provides electric power. The rate of electron flow as measured in amperes.

d *See* penny.

dado joint A joint where a dado or groove is cut in one piece of wood to accept the end of another piece.

dead load The weight of the permanent parts of a structure that must be supported by the other parts of the structure. Does not include the weight of the people, furniture, and other things that occupy the building.

details Drawings used to clarify complicated construction features.

dimension lumber Yard lumber from 2 inches up to and including 4 inches thick and 2 or more inches wide. Includes joists, rafters, studs, plank, and small timbers.

direct-nailing Driving nails so that they are perpendicular to the surface or joint of two pieces of wood. Also called *face-nailing*.

doorjamb The case that surrounds a door. Consists of two upright side pieces called side jambs and a top horizontal piece called a head jamb.

draw request Monthly request by a contractor to be paid for the materials and labor installed into the project during the previous 30 days, to be drawn from the construction loan.

drywall   Panels consisting of a layer of gypsum plaster covered on both sides with paper, used for finishing interior walls and ceilings. Also called *wallboard*, *gypsum wallboard*, and *Sheetrock*, a trade name.

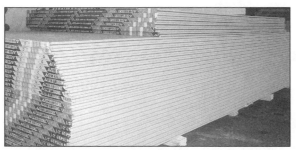

Drywall sheets.

ducts   Pipes that carry air from a furnace or air conditioner to the living areas of a structure.

DWV (drain-waste-vent)   An acronym referring to all or part of the plumbing system that carries waste water from fixtures to the sewer and gases to the roof.

edge grain   Lumber that has been sawed parallel to the pith of the log and approximately at right angles to the growth rings.

elevations   Representational drawings of interior and exterior walls to show finish features.

Elevation plan.

expansion joint   A fiber strip used to separate blocks or units of concrete to prevent cracking due to expansion as a result of temperature changes. Often used on a larger concrete foundation and floor slabs.

face-nailing   Driving nails so that they are perpendicular to the surface or joint of two pieces of wood. Also called *direct-nailing*.

finish carpentry   The fine work—such as that for doors, stairways, and moldings—required to complete a building.

finish electrical work   The installation of the visible parts of the electrical system, such as the fixtures, switches, plugs, and wall plates.

finish plumbing   The installation of the attractive visible parts of a plumbing system such as plumbing fixtures and faucets.

finished basement   A basement that is completed with floor, wall, and ceiling coverings as well as with supporting systems (electrical, plumbing, HVAC).

fire-stop   A solid, tight piece of wood or other material to prevent the spread of fire and smoke. In a frame wall, usually a piece of 2 by 4 cross-blocking between studs.

fitting   In plumbing, any device that connects pipe to pipe or pipe to fixtures.

fixture   In plumbing, any device that is permanently attached to the water system of a house. In electrical work, any lighting device attached to the surface, recessed into, or hanging from the ceiling or walls.

floor plan   A representational drawing of everything that constitutes the house.

footing   The rectangular concrete base that supports a foundation wall or pier or a retaining wall. Usually wider than the structure it supports.

forms   The temporary structure, usually of wood, that supports the shape of poured concrete until it is dry.

foundation The supporting portion of a structure below the first-floor construction or below grade, including the footings.

frame The enclosing woodwork around doors and windows. Also, the skeleton of a building; lies under the interior and exterior wall coverings and roofing.

Interior wood wall frame.

furring strips Narrow strips of wood attached to walls or ceilings; forms a true surface on which to fasten other materials.

fuse A safety device for electrical circuits; interrupts the flow of current when it exceeds predetermined limits for a specific time period.

Screw-in fuse.

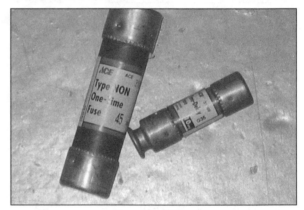

Cartridge fuse.

girder A large beam of steel or wood; supports parts of the structure above it.

grade The ground level surrounding a structure. The natural grade is the original level. The finished grade is the level after the structure is completed.

grain The direction, size, arrangement, appearance, or quality of fibers in wood.

ground Connected to the earth or something serving as the earth, such as a cold-water pipe. The ground wire in an electrical circuit is usually bare or has green insulation.

ground fault circuit interrupter (GFCI) An electrical safety device that senses any shock hazard and shuts off a circuit or receptacle.

grout   Mortar that can flow into the cavities and joints of any masonry work, especially the filling between tiles and concrete blocks.

gypsum wallboard   Panels consisting of a layer of gypsum plaster covered on both sides with paper, used for finishing interior walls and ceilings. Also called *wallboard*, *drywall*, and *Sheetrock*.

hanger   Any of several types of metal devices for supporting pipes, framing members, or other items. Usually referred to by the items they are designed to support—for example, joist hanger or pipe hanger.

hardboard   A synthetic wood panel made by chemically converting wood chips to basic fibers and then forming the panels under heat and pressure. Also called *Masonite*, a brand name.

hardwood   The wood of broadleaf trees, such as maple, oak, and birch. Although hardwood is usually harder than softwood, the term has no actual reference to the hardness of the wood.

header   A horizontal member over a door, window, or other opening; supports the members above it. Usually made of wood, stone, or metal. Also called a *lintel*. Also, in the framing of floor or ceiling openings, a beam used to support the ends of joists.

hot wire   In an electrical circuit, any wire that carries current from the power source to an electrical device. The hot wire is usually identified with black, blue, or red insulation, but it can be any color except white or green.

insulation   Any material that resists the conduction of heat, sound, or electricity.

insulation board   A structural building board made of coarse wood or cane fiber in ½-inch and ²⁵⁄₃₂-inch thicknesses. It can be obtained in various size sheets in various densities, and with several treatments.

interior finish   Any material (wall coverings and trim, for example) used to cover the framing members of the interior of a structure.

jack studs   *See* cripple studs.

jamb   The frame surrounding a door or window; consists of two vertical pieces called side jambs and a top horizontal piece called a head jamb.

joist   One of a series of parallel beams, usually 2 inches in thickness, used to support floor and ceiling loads and supported in turn by larger beams, girders, or bearing walls.

junction box   A metal or plastic container for electrical connections. Sometimes just called a *box*.

kiln-dried lumber   Lumber that has been kiln dried, often to a moisture content of 6 to 12 percent. Common varieties of softwood lumber, such as framing lumber are dried to a somewhat higher moisture content.

laminate   To form a panel or sheet by bonding two or more layers of material. Also, a product formed by such a process—plastic laminate used for countertops, for example.

landing   The platform between flights of stairs or at the end of a stairway.

lath   A building material of metal, gypsum, wood, or other material used as a base on which to apply plaster or stucco.

layout   Any drawing showing the arrangement of structural members or features. Also the act of transferring the arrangement to the site.

level   The position of a vertical line from any place on the surface of the earth to the center of the earth. Also, the horizontal position parallel to the surface of a body of still water. Also a device used to determine when surfaces are level or plumb.

linear measure   Any measurement along a line.

lintel *See* header.

live load All loads on a building not created by the structure of the building itself; the furniture, people, and other things that occupy the building.

lumber A wood product manufactured by sawing, resawing, and passing wood lengthwise through a standard planing machine, and then crosscutting to length.

Lumber.

main drain In plumbing, the pipe that collects the discharge from branch waste lines and carries it to the outer foundation wall, where it connects to the sewer line.

main vent In plumbing, the largest vent pipe to which branch vents may connect. Also called the *vent stack*.

Masonite A brand name for *hardboard*.

masonry Stone, brick, concrete, hollow tile, concrete block, gypsum, block, or other similar building units or materials bonded together with mortar to form a foundation, wall, pier, buttress, or similar mass.

mastic A viscous material used as an adhesive for setting tile or resilient flooring.

miter box A tool that guides a saw in making miter or angle cuts.

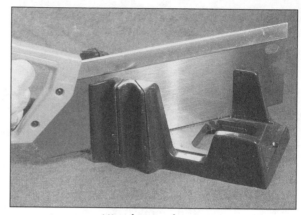

Miter box and saw.

mortar A mixture of sand and Portland cement; used for bonding bricks, blocks, tiles, or stones.

mortgage An agreement between a lender and a buyer using real property as security for the loan.

mudsill The lowest member in the framing of a structure; usually 2-by lumber bolted to the foundation wall on which the floor joists rest. Also called a *sill plate*.

neutral wire In a circuit, any wire that is kept at zero voltage. The neutral wire completes the circuit from source to fixture or appliance to ground. The covering of neutral wires is always white.

newel The main post at the foot of a stairway. Also the central support of a winding or spiral flight of stairs.

nipple In plumbing, any short length of pipe externally threaded on both ends.

NM cable Nonmetallic sheathed electric cable used for indoor wiring. Also known by the brand name *Romex*.

nominal size The size designation of a piece of lumber before it is planed or surfaced. If the actual size of a piece of surfaced lumber is $1\frac{1}{2}$ by $3\frac{1}{2}$ inches, it is referred to by its nominal size: 2 by 4.

nonbearing wall   A wall supporting no load other than its own weight.

nosing   The part of a stair tread that projects over the riser. Also the rounded edge on any board.

on center   Referring to the spacing of joists, studs, rafters, or other structural members as measured from the center of one to the center of the next. Usually written o.c. or OC.

outlet   In a wall, ceiling, or floor, a device into which the plugs on appliance and extension cords are placed to connect them to electric power. Properly called a *receptacle*.

panel   A large, thin board or sheet of construction material. Also a thin piece of wood or plywood in a frame of thicker pieces, as in a panel door or wainscoting.

parquet   A type of wood flooring in which small strips of wood are laid in squares of alternating grain direction. Parquet floors are now available in ready-to-lay blocks to be put down with mastic. Also any floor with an inlaid design of various woods.

Parquet.

particleboard   A form of composite board or panel made of wood chips bonded with adhesive.

partition   A wall that subdivides any room or space within a building.

penny   As applied to nails, it originally indicated the price per hundred. The term now serves as a measure of nail length and is abbreviated by the letter *d*.

Phillips head   A kind of screw and screwdriver on which the diving mechanism is an X rather than a slot.

pier   A column of masonry, usually rectangular, used to support other structural members. Often used as a support under decks.

pigtail   A short length of electrical wire or group of wires.

plan   The representation of any horizontal section of a structure, part of a structure, or the site of a structure; shows the arrangement of the parts in relation and scale to the whole.

plaster   A mixture of lime, sand, and water plus cement for exterior cement plaster, and plaster of paris for interior smooth plaster used to cover the surfaces of a structure.

plasterboard   *See* wallboard.

plate   A horizontal framing member, usually at the bottom or top of a wall or other part of a structure, on which other members rest. The *mudsill*, *soleplate*, and *top plate* are examples.

plumb   Exactly perpendicular; vertical.

plywood   A wood product made up of layers of wood veneer bonded together with adhesive. It is usually made up of an odd number of plies set at a right angle to each other.

Plywood sheets.

post   A vertical support member, usually made up of only one piece of lumber or a metal pipe or I-beam.

putty   A soft, pliable material used for sealing the edges of glass in a sash or to fill small holes or cracks in wood.

PVC (polyvinyl chloride)   A rigid, white, plastic pipe used in plumbing for supply and DWV systems.

quarter-round   A convex molding shaped like a quarter circle when viewed in cross section.

receptacle   In a wall, ceiling, or floor, an electric device into which the plugs on appliance and extension cords are placed to connect them to electric power. Also called an *outlet*.

register   In a wall, floor, or ceiling, the device through which air from the furnace or air conditioner enters a room. Also any device for controlling the flow of heated or cooled air through an opening.

rim joist   *See* band joist.

ripping   Sawing wood in the direction of the grain.

riser   Each of the vertical boards between the treads of a stairway.

Romex   A brand name for nonmetallic sheathed electric cable used for indoor wiring. Also called *NM cable*.

rough-in   To install the basic, hidden parts of a plumbing, electrical, or other system while the structure is in the framing stage. Contrasts with installation of finish electrical work or plumbing, which consists of the visible parts of the system.

run   In stairways, the front-to-back width of a single stair or the horizontal measurement from the bottom riser to the back of the top tread.

section   A drawing of part of a building as it would appear if cut through by a vertical plane.

service panel   The box or panel where the electricity is distributed to the house circuits. It contains the circuit breakers and, usually, the main disconnect switch.

Service panel and circuit breakers.

Sheetrock   A commercial name for *wallboard*.

shim   A thin wedge of wood, often part of a shingle, used to bring parts of a structure into alignment.

shoe molding   A strip of wood used to trim the bottom edge of a baseboard.

shutoff valve   In plumbing, a fitting to shut off the water supply to a single fixture or branch of pipe.

sill plate   The lowest member in the framing of a structure; usually a 2-by board bolted to the foundation wall on which the floor joists rest. Also called a *mudsill*.

site plan   Drawing of all the existing conditions on the lot, usually including slope and other topography, existing utilities, and setbacks. These drawings may be provided by the municipality.

slab   A concrete foundation or floor poured directly on the ground.

sleepers   Boards embedded in or attached to a concrete floor; serve to support and provide a nailing surface for a subfloor or finish flooring.

soffit   The underside of a stairway, cornice, archway, or similar member of a structure. Usually a small area relative to a ceiling.

soil stack   In the DWV system, the main vertical pipe. Usually extends from the basement to a point above the roof.

soleplate   In a stud wall, the bottom member, which is nailed to the subfloor. Also called a *bottom plate*.

solid bridging   A solid member placed between adjacent floor joists near the center of the span to prevent joists from twisting.

span   The distance between structural supports, such as walls, columns, piers, beams, girders, and trusses.

splash block   A small masonry block laid with the top close to the ground surface to receive roof drainage from downspouts and to carry it away from the foundation.

square   A term used to describe an angle of exactly 90 degrees. Also a device to measure such an angle. Also a unit of measure equaling 100 square feet.

stringer   In a stairway, the supporting member to which the treads and risers are fastened. Also called a *carriage*.

strip flooring   Wood flooring consisting of narrow, matched strips.

stucco   A plaster of sand, Portland cement, and lime used to cover the exterior of buildings.

stud   One of a series of wood or metal vertical framing members that are the main units of walls and partitions.

stud wall   The main framing units for walls and partitions in a building, composed of studs; top plates; bottom plates; and the framing of windows, doors, and corner posts.

subfloor   Plywood or oriented strand boards attached to the joists. The finish floor is laid over the subfloor. The subfloor also can be made of concrete.

sump pump   A small capacity pump for occasionally emptying a sump or pit in the floor of a basement.

suspended ceiling   A system for installing ceiling tile by hanging a metal framework from the ceiling joists.

switch   In electrical systems, a device for turning the flow of electricity on and off in a circuit or diverting the current from one circuit to another.

termite shield   Galvanized steel or aluminum sheets placed between the foundation, pipes, or fences and the wood structure of a building; prevents the entry of termites.

threshold   A shaped piece of wood or metal, usually beveled on both edges, that is placed on the finish floor between the side jamb; forms the bottom of an exterior doorway.

timber   Pieces of lumber with a cross section greater than 4 by 6 inches. Usually used as beams, girders, posts, and columns.

toenailing   Driving a nail at a slant to the initial surface in order to permit it to penetrate into a second member.

tongue and groove   A way of milling lumber so that it fits together tightly and forms an extremely strong floor or deck. Also boards milled for tongue-and-groove flooring or decking that have one or more tongues on one edge and a matching groove or grooves on the other.

top plate   In a stud wall, the top horizontal member to which the cap plate is nailed when the stud walls are connected and aligned.

trap   In plumbing, a U-shaped drain fitting that remains full of water to prevent the entry of air and sewer gas into the building

tread   In a stairway, the horizontal surface on which a person steps.

trim   Any finish materials in a structure that are placed to provide decoration or to cover the joints between surfaces or contrasting materials. Door and window casings, baseboards, picture moldings, and cornices are examples of trim.

Tongue-and-groove lumber.

Various trim materials used in residential construction.

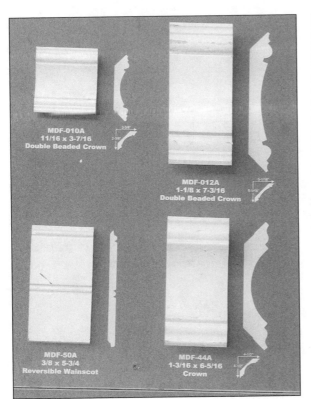

Front and side look at trim.

Vapor barrier.

underlayment The material placed under the finish coverings of floors to provide waterproofing as well as a smooth, even surface on which to apply finish material.

unfinished basement A basement that does not have finished floor, wall, and ceiling coverings, nor supporting systems (electrical, plumbing, HVAC).

vapor barrier Any material used to prevent the penetration of water vapor into walls or other enclosed parts of a building. Polyethylene sheets, aluminum foil, and building paper are the materials used most.

veneer A thin layer of wood, usually one that has beauty or value, that is applied for economy or appearance on top of an inferior surface.

vent Any opening, usually covered with screen or louvers, made to allow the circulation of air, usually into an attic or crawlspace. In plumbing, a pipe in the DWV system for the purpose of bringing air into the system.

vent stack In plumbing, the largest vent pipe to which branch vents may connect. Also called the *main vent*.

walk-out basement The floor of a building partly above and partly below grade. Also known as an American or daylight basement.

wallboard Panels consisting of a layer of gypsum plaster covered on both sides with paper, used for finishing interior walls and ceilings. Also called *gypsum wallboard*, *drywall*, and *Sheetrock*.

water-repellent preservative   A liquid designed to penetrate wood and impart water repellency and a moderate preservative protection.

weather stripping   Narrow strips of metal, fiber, plastic foam, or other materials placed around doors and windows; prevents the entry of air, moisture, or dust.

wire nut   A device that uses mechanical pressure rather than solder to establish a connection between two or more electrical conductors.

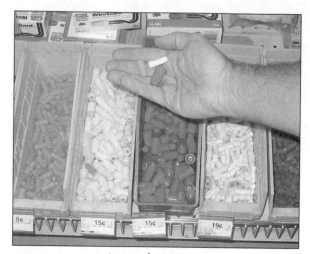

Assorted wire nuts.

Basement Remodeling Resources

This book is written to answer your primary questions about how to remodel your unfinished basement, offering specific options and processes. For additional information on designing, planning, financing, building, and enjoying your finished basement, refer to the 140 resources in this appendix.

The Internet is the best source of current information. It is also widely available in homes, businesses, libraries, and even coffee shops. Therefore, most resources in this appendix refer you to Internet websites that will include up-to-date general and specific information on a wide variety of building topics. Remember to add the prefix "www." to all URLs in this appendix.

Valuable Online Resources

101HomeResources.com
Comprehensive home decorating and building resources directory

BasementIdeas.com
Dave's Dwellings, Inc. of Aurora, Illinois, professional basement remodeling contractor

Build.com
Resource for builders, contractors, remodelers, and do-it-yourselfers

ChiefArchitect.com
Professional drafting and design software by Advanced Relational Technology (ART), Inc.

DoItYourself.com
Wealth of information for all do-it-yourselfers

ECIBuilders.com
ECI Builders of Farmington Hills, Michigan, specializes in basement remodeling

Freeware.com and **Shareware.com**
Free and low-cost software programs

Google.com
Search engine for finding things on the Internet

InsideSpaces.com
For novice home remodelers

MulliganBooks.com
Offering books by Dan Ramsey

PunchSoftware.com
Professional Home Design software by Punch Software

RecRoomFurniture.com
Wide variety of furniture for your recreation room

StartRemodeling.com
Extensive site for everything involving remodeling

Welliner.com
Decorative basement window well murals and lighting

WindowWell.com
Emergency exits for basement bedrooms

YourCompleteHome.com
Home plans and contractor directory

Remodeling and Construction Magazines

Better Homes & Gardens: bhg.com

Builder: builderonline.com

Canadian House & Home: canadianhouseandhome.com

Canadian Living: canadianliving.com

Coastal Living: coastallivingmag.com

Concrete Homes: concretehomesmagazine.com

Country Living: countryliving.com

Environmental Building News: ebuild.com

Fine Homebuilding: finehomebuilding.com

Good Housekeeping: goodhousekeeping.com

Home and Design: homeanddesign.com

House Beautiful: housebeautiful.com

Log Home Living: homebuyerpubs.com

Metal Construction News: moderntrade.com

Natural Home: naturalhomemagazine.com

Permanent Buildings & Foundations: pbf.org

Residential Architect: residentialarchitect.com

Southern Living: southern-living.com

Sunset: sunsetmagazine.com

This Old House: thisoldhouse.com

Traditional Building: traditionalbuilding.com

Wood Design & Building: wood.ca

Books and Videos on Remodeling Basements

Beckstrom, Robert J. *How to Plan and Remodel Attics and Basements*. San Francisco: Ortho Books, 1991.

Beneke, Jeff. *Converting Garages, Attics and Basements*. Menlo Park, Calif.: Sunset Pub. Corp., 2001.

Carpenter, Tim, and Jeff Taylor. *The Basement Book*. New York: Houghton Mifflin, 1996.

Ching, Frank. *Building Construction Illustrated*. Hoboken, N.J.: John Wiley, 2000.

Cornell, Jane. *Remodeling Basements, Attics and Garages*. Upper Saddle River, N.J.: Creative Homeowner, 1999.

Feirer, Mark. *Quick Guide: Basements*. Upper Saddle River, N.J.: Creative Homeowner, 1998.

Finishing Basements and Attics. Minnetonka, Minn.: Creative Pub. Intl., 2000.

Johnson, Dean, and Robin Hartl. *Finishing a Basement* (video). Hometime.com., 1998.

Kardon, Redwood, Michael Casey, and Douglas Hansen. *Code Check: A Field Guide to Building a Safe House*. Newtown, Conn.: Taunton Press, 2000.

National Electrical Code. Quincy, Mass.: National Fire Protection Association, 2001.

National Standard Plumbing Code. Falls Church, Va.: National Association of Plumbing-Heating-Cooling Contractors, 2000.

Marshall, Paula, ed. *Basements: Your Guide to Planning and Remodeling*. Better Homes and Gardens Books, 1999.

Ogershok, Dave. *National Construction Estimator*. Los Angeles: Craftsman Book Co., 2002.

Ramsey, Dan. *Builder's Guide to Barriers*. New York: McGraw-Hill, 1996.

———. *Builder's Guide to Foundations and Floor Framing*. New York: McGraw-Hill, 1995.

———. *The Complete Idiot's Guide to Building Your Own Home*. Indianapolis, Ind.: Alpha Books, 2002.

———. *Hardwood Floors: Installing, Maintaining, and Repairing*. New York: McGraw-Hill, 1991.

———. *Tile Floors: Installing, Maintaining, and Repairing*. New York: McGraw-Hill, 1991.

Tenenbaum, David J. *The Complete Idiot's Guide to Trouble-Free Home Repair*. Indianapolis, Ind.: Alpha Books, 1999.

Books listed here are available through local bookstores or from MulliganBooks.com.

Remodeling Trade Association Resources Online

Air Conditioning Contractors of America: acca.org

American Concrete Institute: aci-int.org

American Hardware Manufacturers Association: ahma.org

American Institute of Architects: aiaonline.com

American Institute of Building Design: aibd.org

American Lighting Association: americanlightingassoc.com

American National Standards Institute: ansi.org

American Society for Testing and Materials: astm.org

American Society of Heating, Refrigerating & Air Conditioning Engineers: ashrae.org

American Society of Interior Designers: asid.org

Americans with Disabilities Act: usdoj.gov/crt/ada/adahom1.htm

Architectural Woodwork Institute: awinet.org

Associated Builders and Contractors: abc.org

Associated General Contractors of America: agc.org

Associated Soil and Foundation Engineers: asfe.org

Association of Home Appliance Manufacturers: aham.org

Brick Institute of America: bia.org

Building Officials and Code Administrators International: bocai.org

California Redwood Association: calredwood.org

Canadian Homebuilders Association: chba.ca/

Canadian Institute of Plumbing and Heating: ciph.com

Canadian Standards Association: csa.ca/

Canadian Window and Door Manufacturers Association: windoorweb.com

Cast Iron Soil Pipe Institute: cispi.org

Composite Panel Association and Composite Wood Council: pbmdf.com

Concrete Reinforcing Steel Institute: crsi.org

Construction Specifications Institute: csinet.org

Contractor License Reference Site: contractors-license.org

The Council of American Building Officials: cabo.org

Energy Efficient Building Association: eeba.org

The Engineered Wood Association: apawood.org

The Gypsum Association: gypsum.org

Hardwood Council: hardwoodcouncil.com

Hardwood Plywood and Veneer Association: erols.com/hpva/

Home Builders Institute: hbi.org

Institute of Electrical and Electronics Engineers: ieee.org

Insulating Concrete Form Association: forms.org

International Conference of Building Officials: icbo.org

International Standard Organization: iso.ch/

National Aggregates Association: nationalaggregates.org

National Air Duct Cleaners Association: nadca.com

National Association of Home Builders: nahb.com

National Association of the Remodeling Industry: nari.org

National Association of Women in Construction: nawic.org

National Concrete Masonry Association: ncma.org

National Electrical Contractors Association: necanet.org

National Electrical Manufacturers Association: nema.org

National Fire Protection Association: nfpa.org

National Hardwood Lumber Association: natlhardwood.org

National Institute of Building Sciences: nibs.org

National Institute of Standards and Technology: nist.gov

National Oak Flooring Manufacturers Association: nofma.org

National Pest Control Association: pestworld.org

National Rural Water Association: nrwa.org

National Stone Association: aggregates.org

National Tile Contractors Association: tile-assn.com

National Wood Flooring Association: woodfloors.org

National Wood Window and Door Association: nwwda.org

North American Insulation Manufacturers Association: naima.org

North American Steel Framing Alliance: steelframingalliance.com

Occupational Safety and Health Administration: osha.gov/

Plumbing, Heating, Cooling Contractors National Association: naphcc.org

Portland Cement Association: concretehomes.com

Remodeling Association: remodelingassociation.com

Sheet Metal and Air Conditioning Contractors National Association: smacna.org

Southern Building Code Congress International: sbcci.org

Southern Forest Products Association: sfpa.org

Southern Pine Council: southernpine.com

Steel Door Institute: wherryassoc.com/steeldoor.org/default.html

Structural Board Association: sba-osb.com

Underwriters Laboratories Inc.: ul.com

Western Red Cedar Lumber Association: cofi.org/WRCLA/

Western Wood Products Association: wwpa.org

Wood Floor Covering Association: wfca.org

Primary Trade Association Addresses

Air Conditioning Contractors of America
1513 16th Street NW
Washington, DC 20036
202-483-9370

American Subcontractors Association
1004 Duke Street
Alexandria, VA 22314
703-684-3450

Associated Builders and Contractors, Inc.
729 15th Street NW
Washington, DC 20006
202-393-2040

Associated Specialty Contractors
7315 Wisconsin Avenue
Bethesda, MD 20814
301-657-3110

Builders Alliance
P.O. Box 20308
Seattle, WA 98102
206-323-1966

Engineering Contractors Association
8310 Florence Avenue
Downey, CA 90240
213-861-0929

Floor Covering Installation Contractors
Association
P.O. Box 2048
Dalton, GA 30722
404-226-5488

General Building Contractors Association
36 South 18th Street
Philadelphia, PA 19103
215-568-7015

Independent Electrical Contractors of America
P.O. Box 10379
Alexandria, VA 22310
703-549-7351

Independent Professional Painting Contractors
Association
P.O. Box 1759
Huntington, NY 11743
516-423-3654

Insulation Contractors Association of America
15819 Crabbs Branch Way
Rockville, MD 20855
301-590-0030

International Remodeling Contractors
Association
P.O. Box 17063
West Hartford, CT 06117
203-233-7442

Mason Contractors Association of America
17W. 601 14th Street
Oak Brook Terrace, IL 60181
708-620-6767

Mechanical Contractors Association of
America
1385 Piccard Drive
Rockville, MD 20832
301-869-5800

Metal Construction Association
1101 14th Street NW
Washington, DC 20005
202-371-1243

National Association of Home Builders of the
United States
15th and M Street NW
Washington, DC 20005
202-822-0200

National Association of Minority Contractors
806 15th Street NW
Washington, DC 20005
202-347-8259

National Association of Plumbing-Heating-
Cooling Contractors
P.O. Box 6808
Falls Church, VA 22046
703-237-8100

National Association of Reinforcing Steel
Contractors
P.O. Box 280
Fairfax, VA 22030
703-591-1870

National Constructors Association
1730 M Street NW
Washington, DC 20036
202-466-8880

National Electrical Contractors Association
7315 Wisconsin Avenue NW
Washington, DC 20014
202-657-3110

National Insulation Contractors Association
99 Canal Center Plaza
Alexandria, VA 22314
703-683-6422

National Tile Contractors Association
P.O. Box 13629
Jackson, MS 39236
601-939-2071

Painting and Decorating Contractors of
America
3913 Old Lee Highway
Fairfax, VA 22030
703-359-0826

Poured Concrete Wall Contractors Association
825 E. 64th Street
Indianapolis, IN 46220
317-253-5655

Professional Construction Estimators
Association
P.O. Box 11626
Charlotte, NC 28220
704-522-6376

Sheet Metal and Air Conditioning Contractors
National Association
4201 Lafayette Center Drive
Chantilly, VA 22021
703-803-2980

Government Resources

**Department of Housing and Urban
Development:** hud.gov

Environmental Protection Agency: epa.gov/

**Federal Home Loan Mortgage
Corporation:** freddiemac.com

Federal Housing Administration:
hud.gov/fha/

Federal Housing Finance Board: fhfb.gov

Federal National Mortgage Association:
fanniemae.com

Small Business Administration: sba.gov

**Veterans Administration Home Loan
Guarantee Program:** homeloans.va.gov

Index